Palgrave Studies in Institutions, Economics and Law

Series Editors
Alain Marciano
University of Montpelier
Montpellier, France

Giovanni Ramello
University of Eastern Piedmont
Alessandria, Italy

Law and Economics is an interdisciplinary field of research that has emerged in recent decades, with research output increasing dramatically and academic programmes in law and economics multiplying. Increasingly, legal cases have an economic dimension and economic matters depend on rules and regulations. Increasingly, economists have realized that "institutions matter" because they influence economic activities. Increasingly, too, economics is used to improve our understanding of how institutions and how legal systems work. This new Palgrave Pivot series studies the intersection between law and economics, and addresses the need for greater interaction between the two disciplines.

More information about this series at
http://www.palgrave.com/gp/series/15241

Koji Domon

An Economic Analysis of Intellectual Property Rights Infringement

Field Studies in Developing Countries

Koji Domon
Waseda University
Tokyo, Japan

Palgrave Studies in Institutions, Economics and Law
ISBN 978-3-319-90465-8   ISBN 978-3-319-90466-5   (eBook)
https://doi.org/10.1007/978-3-319-90466-5

Library of Congress Control Number: 2018939751

© The Editor(s) (if applicable) and The Author(s) 2018
This work is subject to copyright. All rights are solely and exclusively licensed by the Publisher, whether the whole or part of the material is concerned, specifically the rights of translation, reprinting, reuse of illustrations, recitation, broadcasting, reproduction on microfilms or in any other physical way, and transmission or information storage and retrieval, electronic adaptation, computer software, or by similar or dissimilar methodology now known or hereafter developed.
The use of general descriptive names, registered names, trademarks, service marks, etc. in this publication does not imply, even in the absence of a specific statement, that such names are exempt from the relevant protective laws and regulations and therefore free for general use. The publisher, the authors and the editors are safe to assume that the advice and information in this book are believed to be true and accurate at the date of publication. Neither the publisher nor the authors or the editors give a warranty, express or implied, with respect to the material contained herein or for any errors or omissions that may have been made. The publisher remains neutral with regard to jurisdictional claims in published maps and institutional affiliations.

Cover illustration: Pattern adapted from an Indian cotton print produced in the 19th century

Printed on acid-free paper

This Palgrave Pivot imprint is published by the registered company Springer International Publishing AG part of Springer Nature
The registered company address is: Gewerbestrasse 11, 6330 Cham, Switzerland

For Midori

Acknowledgements

I am grateful to a number of people who have generously supported me. Without local assistants, guides, and members of project teams, I would not have accomplished this long-term research. I wish to sincerely thank Tran Dinh Lam, Michael Yuan, and Giovanni Ramello, who travelled in Asia and held conferences and seminars with me. Discussions with them during the travels stimulated and relaxed my brain. I thank Kiyoshi Nakamura, Nobuko Kawashima, May Sai Thi, and Yasuo Ohkuma for helping me in my field research. The Center for Vietnamese and Southeast Asian Studies at Vietnam National University in Ho Chi Minh City has also supported me in arranging field research for a decade. An anonymous referee and editor of this book series helped me revise the manuscript, and Thane Doss and Joseph Johnson edited it in detail. I would like to thank all of them, but any final errors are my responsibility.

Finally, this publication was financially supported by a Waseda University Grant for Special Research Projects (Project number: 2017K-270, 2017B-268), a Waseda University English Academic Book Publication Support Subsidy in 2017, and a grant from the Policy Research Institute of the Ministry of Agriculture, Forestry and Fisheries in Japan.

CONTENTS

1	Introduction: A Methodology and Its Precursors	1
2	Unauthorized Copying and Incentives for Musicians	11
3	Fake Spare Parts When No Domestic Brand Names Can Be Trusted	35
4	Markets of Quasi-Credence and Similar Foods	61
5	General Conclusions	85
	Index	89

LIST OF FIGURES

Fig. 2.1	A dilemma of musicians	23
Fig. 2.2	Content acquisition method (multiple answers)	27
Fig. 2.3	Main location for Internet use (multiple answers)	28
Fig. 2.4	Internet access speed	29
Fig. 2.5	Frequency distribution of number of illegal CDs	30
Fig. 2.6	Frequency distribution of number of original CDs	30
Fig. 3.1	Market for famous fake brand-name products versus original-name domestic products	41
Fig. 3.2	Market equilibrium under experience goods	45
Fig. 3.3	Demand structure of counterfeiting game	49
Fig. 4.1	Structure of incomplete information	65
Fig. 4.2	Market equilibrium under quasi-credence food	68
Fig. 4.3	Market equilibrium for experience foods	70
Fig. 4.4	Area of demand expansion	75
Fig. 4.5	Percentage of Japanese staff	78
Fig. 4.6	Ownership of Japanese restaurants	78
Fig. 4.7	Channels of ingredient procurement	79
Fig. 4.8	Problems regarding Japanese ingredients	79

CHAPTER 1

Introduction:
A Methodology and Its Precursors

Abstract This chapter explains the importance of considerations of IPR infringement in developing and emerging countries and the necessity of Law and Economics incorporating Industrial Economics into these analyses. Next, a three-step method of field research is explained: first, purchasing illicit goods as a customer in the marketplace; second, conducting interviews with retailers, producers, and consumers; and third, collecting samples from consumers. Main results of the following chapters are summarized, and finally, the possible criticism that the methodology is biased towards an economic perspective is discussed. Accurate legal consideration is important when addressing cases in developed countries. However, in developing countries, with little legal enforcement, addressing IPR infringement requires that we understand the economic reasoning behind phenomena causing it.

Keywords Industrial organization · Law and economics · Methodology of field research

© The Author(s) 2018
K. Domon, *An Economic Analysis of Intellectual Property Rights Infringement*, Palgrave Studies in Institutions, Economics and Law, https://doi.org/10.1007/978-3-319-90466-5_1

1.1 Intellectual Property Rights (IPR) Infringement and Economic Development

Before the housing bubble in the USA burst in 2008–2009, economists believed that the BRICs countries would play a great role in the world economy in this century. As the share of BRICs and other emerging and developing countries in the world economy rose, IPR infringement in these countries received increasing attention, since demand in their domestic markets could no longer be neglected by developed countries. Counterfeit exports from China to other countries increased, with about 80% of counterfeits in ASEAN produced in China, according to the Japan External Trade Organization (JETRO).[1] Even though economic growth in the BRICs and other emerging and developing countries is now weak, and the economists' forecast seems proven wrong, their domestic markets still have influence on the world economy.

Intellectual property rights collectively play a strategically important role in international competition in both developed and developing countries, a role increasing in importance after the economies of the BRICs began to develop. In recent decades, the USA has repeatedly pressed China to protect IPRs, often through the activities[2] of the United States Trade Representative (USTR), and rights holders in developed countries have had many complaints about IPR infringement in emerging and developing countries. While such pressure is necessary to fair competition, infringing countries also strategically make decisions about law enforcement that may seem contradictory to membership in the World Trade Organization (WTO). If a country sees greater benefit from lax or no enforcement than potential damage stemming from political pressure, there is little incentive for strict enforcement of international laws. This is a case that arises with some regularity in emerging and developing countries. Their interests are best served by protecting IPRs only if domestic consumers and producers benefit as a whole from the protection.

In order for developed countries to consider effective methods of protecting their IPRs from infringement in emerging and developing

---

[1] See Ohkuma (2013) regarding data of counterfeit exports in Asia. I was also told, in an interview in Mexico, that Chinese counterfeits smuggled into Mexico by ship container had destroyed the market for domestic counterfeiters in an international battle of counterfeiters.

[2] Based on Section 301 of the US Trade Act of 1974.

countries, they first must understand what is happening on the ground. Mere emotional and political insistence on the necessity of protection cannot effectively protect IPRs. In this monograph, we will examine real markets in which producers and consumers conduct trade. Behind the trade, various incentives well adapted to market situations without IPR enforcement exist. We must reconsider the idea that a market does not "work well" in such situations.

1.2   LAW AND ECONOMICS AND INDUSTRIAL ORGANIZATION

In 1968, G. S. Becker's article "Crime and Punishment: An Economic Approach" introduced economics into the field of law, presenting a comprehensive consideration of crime within an economic model. His considerations included almost all the factors affecting a crime, focusing on the incentives affecting criminals, and contributed to the creation of a new field, Law and Economics (LE). Prior to Becker, Coase (1960) had presented an economic consideration of social cost, which has become one of the seminal works in LE. A much earlier Coase article (1937), which presented a treatment of the economics of transaction cost, seems to have had a greater impact than the 1960 article, as it has many applications beyond the legal. For instance, this article relates to discussions about IPR infringement in the Internet era. The new field of Industrial Organization (IO) also emerged in the 1960s. Two scholars, Bain (1959) and Stigler (1968), published books on IO, helping to popularize the field. In these books, simple data and concrete examples were used as the bases for a theory, similar to the development of LE.

When we consider IPRs, protection of creators from competitors or free riders must be taken into account, and infringement of IPRs is a source of profit in the marketplace. Unlike crimes such as murder and theft, IPR infringement takes place as part of market competition. Therefore, in order to address IPRs fully, LE needs to incorporate IO into its analyses. However, economics researchers are likely to be interested in a unique result, whether it is important for actual policymaking or not, while legal analyses need to be more realistic and to cope with concrete cases. Researchers in LE must position themselves between the two fields, taking into account various factors which economics assumes as given in its model analyses. In the 1980s, theories of IO were rewritten by game theory, as seen in Tirole (1988), and discussions of IPRs

4 K. DOMON

in LE have been also influenced by this trend.[3] Key papers concerning copyright and credence products referenced in Chapters 2 and 4 of this monograph make use of game theory; focusing on competition and pricing, these look like discussions in IO. While they are theoretically interesting, they are too abstract for LE to use when considering concrete cases.

This monograph is based on IO, taking into account actual situations in local markets on which I have performed field research, beginning in 2005. In theoretical analysis, the realistic nature of one's assumptions is important. Assumptions that simplify but are unconvincing are of little value, and it can be difficult to make one's assumptions convincing. Nonetheless, theorists may make assumptions based on analogy to their prior experience, relying on vague impressions in the absence of empirical data. In such situations, a range of discussions, each biased by its assumptions, may emerge; the degree to which our understanding of real situations is clarified and the degree to which it is obscured by these assumptions may be unclear. For example, when we can see that a factor influences a certain phenomenon, a proposition may be obtained under ceteris paribus, but the factor's real impact on the phenomenon may remain vague. We often see such discussions in theoretical IO. Although we cannot take into account all factors affecting phenomena, it is not constructive to emphasize minor factors, satisfied that they lead to interesting propositions, if we seek to analyse and understand actual markets.

1.3   METHODOLOGY OF FIELD RESEARCH

Systems and methods for gathering official statistics concerning market data in developing countries are often immature. In particular, few data concerning IPR infringement can be found because of lax enforcement. Associations such as the Recording Industry Association of America (RIAA) watch for infringement and collect data, but their data are likely to be overestimated and do little to illuminate the situations creating infringers' incentives to break laws. Furthermore, the logic derived from situations in developed countries is often not applicable to developing countries, as Banerjee and Duflo (2011) have described, using many

---

[3] See Miceli (1997) regarding recent theoretical LE.

examples, since researchers in developed countries have rarely experienced and seen actual market trade under conditions of lax enforcement. Our imaginations are very limited.

With a dearth of official data and experience in the marketplace, what researchers can do in order to strengthen understanding of IPR infringement under such conditions is to undertake field research. Although there is no standard method for such research, researchers in development economics have created a method for performing field research that targets developing countries. I naturally and unintentionally used the method when I was eager to understand real markets for illegal products. My activity was limited by research funds, but I found interesting phenomena from interviewing and providing questionnaires to persons participating at various levels in markets characterized by a large amount of illegal behaviour.

My usual method was as follows. First, I purchased illegal products as a customer, using local guides in several markets. In developing countries, illegal products are easily accessible to ordinary people, unlike in developed countries. From this experience, we can realize how consumers interact with illegal products. Without this experience, a simple assumption that only grasps one characteristic among many factors can greatly influence considerations and exaggerate their outcomes. For example, the assumption that consumers are either deceived or not is necessary, but the assumption is too simple to comprehend actual trade in real markets, as will be seen in subsequent chapters.

Second, I interviewed consumers, retailers, producers, wholesalers, and authorities. In order to understand the incentives of each agent, experiencing one position within a market is not enough. It is a useful first step but is likely to cause a bias of considerations if not augmented. A series of interviews is useful to remedy such a bias. We need to see several interviewees and find common opinions, but we must be careful about information credibility. For example, in interviews with Japanese food wholesalers and distributors, some interviewees apparently hid information and told lies, since they were afraid of my relationship with authorities. To get information that is as credible as possible, a trustworthy human network of local guides and assistants is necessary, and information consistency on both supply and demand sides must be checked. Because of illegality, those who are involved in supplying counterfeits are not inclined to talk honestly about their behaviours. I checked their information by comparing it with consumers' and retailers' information.

6   K. DOMON

Third, I collected data by questionnaire. Since it is difficult to collect sample data from producers and distributors inclined to hide illegal trades, these data only concern the demand side. When tracing products through a distribution channel, who is and who is not cheating customers is not an easy problem, and in general, only the final customer has no incentive to hide information. The sample data can be used to ascertain whether propositions we make from our market experiences and interviews are convincing or not. Even if the number of samples is too small for statistical analysis due to budget constraints, we can identify some simple characteristics that we might miss without data.

Field research is a method usually used in anthropology and sociology. Lofland and Lofland (1994) and Sato (2002) explain techniques for interviewing and taking notes in ways that prevent bias. However, compared to the models and statistical analyses of economics, field research lacks a standard method and is dependent on the topic and subject. Sato (2002) insists that eliminating stereotypes is important but not easy, since clear, objective evidence and data do not exist. Under such conditions, researchers are tempted to retain stereotypes they held before field research. To avoid this problem, we need to collect various information and materials, including qualitative evidence, to convince ourselves and eliminate prejudice.[4]

When I started field research on music piracy in 2006, I just took short notes about impressive facts, for example, that musicians need pirated CDs, that finding CD shops dealing only in original CDs is very difficult, that price differences between original and pirated CDs are not large, and so on. Studying how to do field research step by step on the spot, I took pictures and videos to reinforce my memory and provide subjective data, since written notes provide inadequate records of the atmosphere of shops and demeanour of sellers and customers in the marketplace, things that cannot be reflected in any numerical data. Before I collected sample data by questionnaire, I did field research in the marketplace of each country. Without the field research to provide context, interpretations of data would be different and vague.

After my research on music piracy, I initiated research on counterfeit spare parts in 2011. At that time, I hired local assistants to take notes and pictures and always wrote daily reports with them after field

---

[4] See Helper (2000) for a short discussion of field research in economics.

research. I became accustomed to field research, and then, I started research on counterfeit food in 2013. In this research, I wrote detailed notes with many pictures, summarizing it as in field reports. These notes, summaries, and pictures are not directly used in this monograph, but are reflected in model analyses. This style is different from that of field research in anthropology and sociology, in which field reports provide the main descriptions.

1.4 Summary of Outcomes

A thumbnail sketch of the outcomes of my field research and analyses is as follows. Chapter 2 considers music piracy, showing that illegal music CDs have a promotional effect on musician's profits. Since P2P file-sharing became common, this phenomenon has been indicated by researchers analysing the music industry in developed countries. The primary source of musicians' revenues in developed countries has shifted from CDs and other media (back) towards live performance. Under almost no copyright protection, musicians in developing countries have *always* depended on live performance. I theoretically analyse this phenomenon, considering conditions for profit maximization. Next, by using sample data collected in Taiwan, Vietnam, South Korea, China, and Japan, I show a difference among these countries regarding selection of medium. P2P file-sharing was unknown to college students in Vietnam (at the time of my research), while Chinese and Korean students utilized it to download music files. This phenomenon was explained by differences in the maturity of local infrastructure. A relatively high cost for Internet use prevented Vietnamese students from using P2P file-sharing. They stuck to an old medium, pirated CDs. An interesting common phenomenon in all countries was that students bought similar numbers of original CDs by their favourite musicians.

Chapter 3 addresses fake spare parts for motorcycles as trademark infringement. In Southeast Asia, the motorcycle is very popular due to lack of public transportation. In daily life, Southeast Asians care for their motorcycles as Americans care for their automobiles. We can see many packages infringing the trademarks of famous brand names, and we might think that consumers are being cheated. The reality is not so simple, as most consumers do not trust the information on the packages and instead seek and follow the advice given by repair shops. An interesting fact is that consumers do not trust domestic brands more than fake packages. Analysis

8 K. DOMON

of the situation proves that lax enforcement of trademark infringement is better for the local economy than strict enforcement under which foreign brands make more profit. In field research, I ascertained a market transition in which unknown brands producing second-tier quality products gradually penetrated into the market as consumers' incomes increased. I theoretically considered the possibility that producers of second-tier quality products were forced to counterfeit a trademark due to competition with counterfeiters producing third-tier products. In the end, all counterfeiters do not always prefer lax enforcement.

Chapter 4 considers fake food infringing trademarks and design rights. Genetically modified foods, classified as credence goods in economics, are almost impossible for consumers to detect if counterfeit, and judgment of their quality is problematic. Foreign foods for local consumers have a similar property, since these consumers rarely, if ever, eat authentic foreign food. Field research in Thailand, Indonesia, and Vietnam shows that cheap local restaurants' owners and chefs also often lack enough experience to judge authenticity. Therefore, not only customers but also restaurants can be deceived by vicious wholesalers and traders. In such situations, the quality of counterfeit foreign food is overestimated, but local consumers cannot know this. Lacking experience with non-counterfeit foods, their faulty evaluation does not matter because they are satisfied with the food. Establishing fair competition between original producers and counterfeiters is problematic. I indicate that domestic social welfare may decrease with overestimation only if the producer of originals is domestic. Authorities in developing countries therefore have an incentive for strict enforcement. I also consider imitated food from the perspective of biological mimicry. There are plenty of imitations of well-known foreign foods whose status as instances of legal infringement is unclear. Illegality depends at least partly upon the demerits of an imitation for an original producer. Biological evolution shows that imitations or mimics can be beneficial to an original. I investigate how this possibility applies to a model of product differentiation.

1.5 CONCLUDING REMARKS

The methodology described in this monograph is unique and seems to be controversial among researchers of LE and IO. Criticisms include that my considerations do not address legal matters comprehensively enough and that my empirical analyses provide too little data to provide robust statistics. These are just criticisms, and considerable room for improvement exists. However, in spite of these shortcomings, I believe the rationale motivating this work has value, as field research reveals facts whose importance is neglected or goes unnoticed; though some may feel that such socio-economic factors lie outside the scope of the fields of LE and IO, I would assert that these fields are embedded in a matrix of socio-economic factors without which they would have little explanatory value.

Legal scholars have argued that my descriptions of what is counterfeit are somewhat vague. While I've not done the type of scientific testing that would be desirable in a court of law, in contrast to developed countries, in the countries where I did research counterfeits are obvious from the marketplaces in which they are sold and from their price levels. The lack of scientific testing of specific items detracts little from the assessments found in my research.

REFERENCES

Bain, J. S. (1959). *Industrial Organization*. New York: Wiley.

Banerjee, A. V., & Duflo, E. 2011. *Poor Economics: A Radical Rethinking of the Way to Fight Global Poverty*, Public Affairs.

Becker, G. S. (1968). Crime and Punishment: An Economic Approach. *Journal of Political Economy, 76*(2), 169–217.

Coase, R. H. (1937). The Nature of the Firm. *Economica, 4*(16), 386–405.

Coase, R. H. (1960). The Problem of Social Cost. *Journal of Law and Economics, 3*, 1–44.

Helper, S. (2000). Economists and Field Research: You Can Observe a Lot Just by Watching. *American Economic Review, 90*(2), 228–232.

Lofland, J., & Lofland, L. H. (1994). *Analyzing Social Settings: A Guide to Qualitative Observation and Analysis* (3rd ed.). Belmont, CA: Wadsworth Publishing Company.

Miceli, T. J. (1997). *Economics of the Law: Torts, Contracts, Property, Litigation*. New York: Oxford University Press.

Ohkuma, S. (2013). Some IP Issues in ASEAN. In K. Domon, T. Dinh Lam, & S. Kaur (Eds.), *Intellectual Property Rights in Developing Countries: Conference Proceedings, Vietnam 2012* (pp. 101–123). Ho Chi Minh, Vietnam: VNU-HCM Publishing House.

Sato, I. (2002). *Fiirudo Whaku no Giho: Toi wo Sodateru Kasetsu wo Kitaeru* (in Japanese), Shinyosha.

Stigler, J. G. (1968). *The Organization of Industry*. Homewood, IL: Richard D. Irwin, Inc.

Tirole J. 1988. *The Theory of Industrial Organization*. Cambridge and London: MIT Press.

CHAPTER 2

Unauthorized Copying and Incentives for Musicians

Abstract This chapter considers piracy in the music industry. After identifying general factors influencing music piracy, using facts obtained by field research, I analyse reasons why P2P file-sharing was rare in Vietnam and show that piracy worked as necessary free promotion of live performance for most musicians. I also provide a theoretical analysis considering the condition of profit maximization using piracy as promotion. Furthermore, using samples collected from college students in Japan, China, Vietnam, and South Korea, I consider how music piracy is impacted by transaction costs: ISP fees, risk of apprehension, time to download files, etc. Each country has unique characteristics which can be explained by its transaction costs. I explain these characteristics by using the Cobb–Douglas utility function.

Keywords Music piracy · P2P file-sharing · Transaction cost

This section modifies and extends discussion of Domon and Nakamura (2007) and Domon and Lam (2009).

© The Author(s) 2018
K. Domon, *An Economic Analysis of Intellectual Property Rights Infringement*, Palgrave Studies in Institutions, Economics and Law,
https://doi.org/10.1007/978-3-319-90466-5_2

11

2.1 Background

At the end of last century, the appearance of Napster raised the controversial problem of file-sharing on the Internet. The service created a website at which users could upload and/or download any music track file, without charge, for sharing. Before the service started, the doctrine of fair or personal use of music content legally allowed content holders to share copies among friends and to copy original music tracks for personal use. When a de facto standard data compression format, MP3, prevailed throughout the world, consumers, most often teens and college students, could share compatible copies of MP3 files for portable music player use. In this situation, development in high-speed access, like Asymmetric Digital Subscriber Line (ADSL), supported file-sharing on the Internet. At the same time, recording companies started to introduce online distribution services for music files.[1]

In court, Napster lost when it was sued for illegal copying, and it ceased file-sharing. However, in addition to Napster, a P2P (peer-to-peer) software network called Gnutella and its subspecies had become widespread early in the millennium. Because its software used each user's PC to store files for file-sharing, it was physically impossible to stop file-sharing by the software. Efforts to combat P2P arose. Japan,[2] for example, enacted new laws to restrict personal copying, banning both uploading and downloading copyrighted content in the public domain. However, illegal file-sharing persisted there, and it persists today, though the number of P2P users is decreasing compared to a decade and a half ago.

After the emergence of Gnutella, there were many discussions about the effects of P2P on music CD sales. Recording companies and musicians insisted that a decrease in CD sales and revenues was caused by P2P, while the opponents said that P2P had a promotional effect on CD sales, and the decrease in CD sales resulted from a change in lifestyle, which, relative to previous habits, devalued music's utility. Since online music services like i-Tunes and Spotify have launched and succeeded,

---

[1] For example, in 2000, 10 major Japanese labels made a common DRM (digital rights management) system and opened websites for an online download service. However, the service was not popular.

[2] A popular P2P file-sharing software in Japan, called Winny, triggered discussion of how to combat illegal file-sharing. The developer was sued in Japan, but finally found not guilty. Many software developers argued by analogy that Winny did not cause illegal copying any more than a knife causes murder.

such discussions have gradually disappeared, and a shift in relative importance of revenue sources of recording companies and musicians has taken place, from CDs to online downloads, ticket sales, and advertisements on YouTube and other websites.

The above history of the music industry in recent times describes the situation in developed countries, where almost all people can access broadband Internet. We should remember that the popularity of P2P was dependent upon such telecommunication infrastructure. However, piracy of digital goods was already widespread in the developing countries of Asia before P2P was considered a serious problem in developed countries. Around 2005, P2P was gradually penetrating the population of college students in Japan who had been unable to access a wide range of pirated CDs before. In those days, I suspected that college students in other Asian countries also used P2P, and I investigated to make sure.

I used field studies methods, collecting questionnaires on campus, interviewing college students, musicians, and recording companies, and visiting black markets. My selected countries were Japan, Vietnam, China, and South Korea. I collected questionnaires in 2006. Interviews and research in black markets were conducted from 2006 to 2008, after data collection. Although these dates may seem old, it is important that the work was done as the primary medium used in the music industry was shifting from the CD to online downloading. Apple's iTune Music Store, which triggered serious growth in download services, opened in the USA in 2003, in some countries of the EU in 2004, and in Japan in 2005. YouTube also began service in 2005, creating a new style of watching music for free via online videos. Therefore, a critical turning point occurred around 2005, the year when I started this research. In order to study the impact of online digitalization in the music industry upon piracy, and the impact of a media shift upon piracy in general, the timing was opportune.

I focused especially on Vietnam, where there was almost no enforcement and the piracy rate was the highest among the four countries I studied. Interviews and research concerning black markets were performed mainly in Vietnam, where I found phenomena that researchers in developed countries could not observe. Merely from data surveys, we cannot correctly assess the impacts of socio-economic differences among countries on piracy. Field studies using interviews and research in black markets can cover this shortcoming. There are three parts of a market to investigate: the demand side, the supply side, and the trade in the marketplace. The demand side can be examined by data surveys and interviews of college students, the supply side by interviews with musicians and recording companies, and trade in the marketplace by interviewing personnel at illegal CD stores. These basic components interact with each other in a market.

2.2   RELATED LITERATURE

A first boom of discourse concerning copying and copyright problems began in the 1980s, as the photocopy machine and video cassette recorder (VCR) became widely available for personal use. In the USA, whether fair use was applicable to such personal copying was discussed in court and academia. Relative to our topic, Gordon's discussion (1982) at that time is instructive. She argued that personal copying of TV programs by VCR did not impact the market due to the high transaction cost of supplying such copies to the market. Since a video cassette market of TV programs could not only exist but also could be created, she insisted that personal copying by VCR was fair use. That is, if the utility stemming from personal copying could not be commercialized, that copying would be fair use. If utility from a copyable product is increased by personal copying in an already existing market, Leibovitz (1985) argued that price discrimination by consumers constituted proper pricing. His point is that the value of a product is variable according to the use, and copying is one such a use. If a producer can precisely monitor use and control use, she or he discriminates price according to the way a product is used. Only when the transaction cost of such monitoring and control is very high does price discrimination become impossible for most products, making them essentially free to use for consumers.

A key factor of the above discussion is transaction cost, which has decreased with new technology and innovation. After the VCR became commonplace, a new, profitable market emerged for the film industry, which began to supply movie videos, especially for video rental shops. This second use of films became a major source of the film industry's profits. Without fair use treatment of the copying of TV programs, this business could not have been created. This suggests that a decrease in transaction cost is first utilized by consumers for personal duplication. Second, a producer tries to strip consumers of the benefit by pricing, taking into account transaction cost. Third, there is the possibility of creating a new market based on a new copy technology.

Before P2P file-sharing became popular, there were discussions that considered copyable products as club goods, shared among a group. Besen and Kirby (1989) analysed the situation by simulation, taking into account the transaction cost for sharing in a group. In the simulation, whether social welfare increased or not was ambiguous, depending upon copying and the cost of forming a group. Varian (2000) also considered a sharing and copying problem in a simple linear model, showing that both consumers and the producer are better off if transaction costs are relatively low compared to production costs. A similar result was obtained as to price discrimination under incomplete information by Domon (2006). According to Varian (2005), these considerations are not appropriate for file-sharing on the Internet, where transaction costs are nearly zero.

The problem of file-sharing emerged after content digitalization drastically decreased the cost of copying by personal computer in the 1990s. In 1999, Napster, with a sharing cost of nearly zero, triggered debate concerning whether file-sharing decreased CD sales or not. In real markets, CD sales were affected by many factors, which were classified as substitute, complement, demographic, and other socio-economic effects. As Andersen and Frenz (2010) summarized and explained, P2P file-sharing played a role in sampling and discovering musical tracks to which consumers had not listened, ultimately leading to CD purchases, while there were also consumers substituting for CD purchases with music files obtained by free file-sharing. They argued that net change in the rate of CD sales was dependent upon which is greater, an increase caused by sampling or a decrease by displacement, and said that there was no clear relationship between CD sales and P2P file-sharing. Thereafter, Barker and Maloney (2015) critically amended the analysis of Andersen and Frenz (2010), insisting that a positive relationship existed between CD sales' declining and P2P file-sharing. Liebowitz (2016) compared relationships obtained in 12 papers, examining the range of coefficients, and found shortcomings in other papers, including Andersen and Frenz (2010), concluding that none had demonstrated an absence of harm to sales due to copying.

The relationship between CD sales and P2P file-sharing is a controversial issue. However, for musicians (in contrast to recording companies), total revenues from music activities are more important than CD sales. Musicians have many sources of revenue from music other than CD sales: royalties from use in advertisements and by other artists, live concert performances, music videos, and so on. Data about live concert performance in the USA collected by Mortimer et al. (2012) suggested that demand for live performance by lesser-known and middle-level musicians was increased due to a promotion effect of P2P file-sharing. This is suggestive when considering the music industry in developing countries. Varian (2005) also referred to the possibility of a promotional effect of pirated songs under no enforcement.

The above literature considered situations in developed countries with strict law enforcement. Since illegal file-sharing is occurring in developed countries with failed enforcement, it has been a focus of interest for many researchers. However, there are few researchers interested in file-sharing and illegal copying in developing countries. We find no such papers in databases such as EconLit. Contributing factors to this lack of attention are the absence of copyright enforcement and of official and reliable market data in these settings, but we can use them to illuminate what happens without law enforcement, a situation that has not been present in developed countries since the nineteenth century.

2.3 Factors Causing P2P File-Sharing Expansion in Developed Countries

Before comparing P2P file-sharing between developed and developing countries, we consider factors that make it beneficial in developed countries. P2P file-sharing incurs the following costs:

1. Time to search and download: This opportunity cost is a major factor affecting the efficiency of P2P file-sharing, since the Internet drastically reduces this cost. Before online download services of music tracks were available, CDs had to be purchased at a store or on the street. The transportation costs and time spent were not negligible. If consumers did not mind the lack of a jacket and accompanying text, P2P file-sharing saved time as well as money.
2. Risk of apprehension: There is a risk of being apprehended. The probability is extremely low, compared to other illegal situations. However, indictments against P2P users have been effective in reducing the number of such users, although there are still many. Each user considers the expected damages if he/she is apprehended, and decides whether to use P2P file-sharing or not.

3. Low quality: To share files efficiently on the Internet, they are compressed in size, to, for example, about 1/10th by the MP3 format. However, the sound of compressed files is degraded. The extent of the degradation is dependent on the method of compression.

How these factors affect a user depends on his/her characteristics. Since college students, for example, have relatively large amounts of free time, their opportunity costs are low. Their damage from apprehension is also lower than that of full-time workers. Comparing these costs with prices in stores, users decide whether or not to use P2P file-sharing.[3]

To compete with P2P file-sharing, major labels began to sell music files online at lower prices than physical copies than in stores. Price is another important factor to analyse as an advantage of P2P file-sharing. In addition, portable hard disc players or smartphones accelerated online sales, quickly making CDs an old-fashioned medium.

In developed countries, the spread of P2P file-sharing depends upon both transaction costs and online prices.[4] As online download services become common, the number of P2P file-sharing users decreases due to low online prices and no transportation costs to purchase a music file. P2P file-sharing becomes a competitor of downloading services.

In the next sections, I will examine to what extent these relationships held in developing countries where copyright protection was very lax, at the time when P2P became a serious social issue, around 2005. It is important to consider the situation that users faced in terms of telecommunication services and infrastructure, as well as copyright protection. These factors significantly influenced transaction costs for P2P file-sharing.

---

[3] Domon and Yamazaki (2004) considered the pricing of digital content in such a situation.

[4] Major labels have introducing DRM, which controls how content purchased in the market may be used. Typically, it relies upon a copy control CD, which does not allow physical copying of content. In Japan this failed, since many consumers did not accept the system. Meanwhile, online stores have devised flexible menus of DRM that do not restrict private copying in the same way as a copy control CD. When we consider the merits derived from purchased content, DRM is an important factor.

2.4 Circumstances for P2P File-Sharing in Vietnam

To investigate P2P file-sharing in developing countries, I selected Vietnam for field study. This country was notorious for infringement of intellectual property rights and was on the Watch List of the US Special 301 Report. I first visited the country in September of 2005, and I conducted field research 5 times between then and 2008. Research was centred in Ho Chi Minh City (HCMC), the biggest city in Vietnam. I investigated CD stores and Internet cafes and interviewed college students, shoppers, and musicians. During this field research, I also collected sample data from college students, which will be discussed later.

Before proceeding, I should describe the general economic situation at that time. Nominal Vietnamese GDP per capita in 2005 was US$700 according to IMF statistics, but annual income in HCMC was higher than that. According to our interviews, the average monthly salary of workers in HCMC was about US$100 in those days. The university entrance rate in Vietnam was 16% in 2005, according to the UNESCO Institute of Statistics. These data greatly differed from those of developed countries.

I first investigated CD stores. There were two ways to purchase CDs and DVDs[5] in Vietnam. The more popular one was to purchase pirated CDs. Stores selling such CDs were all over HCMC when we did our research. This suggests that authorities were implementing few measures to protect copyright.[6] Prices of a pirated CD and DVD were, respectively, 12,000 Vietnamese Dong (US$0.80) or 17,000 Vietnamese Dong (US$1.13)[7] at most stores. An interesting phenomenon was that large pirate stores also sold copyrighted content. When popular pirated CDs, listed in contemporary hit-charts, were sold out, people had to purchase the copyrighted ones.[8] In HCMC, a store dealing only in original CDs was very difficult to find. There were only two such stores, both owned by the state. Private CD stores sold both original and pirated CDs. That

[5] Another medium, the VCD, remains in Vietnam. It is a movie whose screen quality is worse than that of a DVD. Due to its low price, it was common in Vietnam.

[6] The authorities have made efforts to get rid of piracy, but with little impact on the pirate markets. See reports in http://www.phamassociates.com.vn/English/Index.htm.

[7] The price level in HCMC was about one-tenth that of Tokyo.

[8] Most CD stores procured pirated CDs from wholesalers and did not produce them for themselves because production cost within the store was high.

is, pirated and legal content coexisted in the market with differentiation from each other.

This coexistence indicates that copyright enforcement did not work well in Vietnam. In fact, authorities rarely protected the copyrights of either domestic or foreign content. However, a price system worked under this situation. The first difference between a pirated and a copyrighted CD was in the package. The jacket of a pirated CD was a thin colour copy of the original and carried no written lyrics. The second difference was in quality. Pirated CDs were often imperfectly copied. The price of a copyrighted CD was 32,000 Vietnamese Dong (US$2.13), about two-and-a-half times as high as that of a pirated one. The Vietnamese sometimes purchased a copyrighted CD when it was a favourite, or as a gift.

Various kinds of domestic music had also been supplied for the market, in spite of the almost non-existent copyright protection. This suggests that musicians in Vietnam earned their main incomes from concert performances. CD sales, including pirated CDs, contributed to promotion for live concerts.

I checked Internet access fees and the prices of PCs. Fees for Internet access can significantly influence the extent of P2P file-sharing. Even if the Internet is available, people do not use it if access fees are high. There were three services available for home use of the Internet: dial-up, ISDN, and DSL.[9] Internet cafes also provided access to the Internet at a rate of about 20 cents per hour. The cheapest access was at an Internet cafe, since dial-up access services at home cost about 60 cents per hour. The average cost to use ADSL at home was about US$20 per month, which was expensive in Vietnam. Another problem in using the Internet was the speed (bandwidth) of networks. The average speed was about 100 kbps at an Internet cafe, where people could easily have access to the Internet. The speed at home was similar to or less than 100 kbps. Therefore, the real fee per bps was very high in Vietnam compared to an average income. Yet another problem when people used the Internet at home was the price of PCs, which was roughly the same as in developed countries.

---

[9] In 2001, Internet access service was opened to the private sector. There are several major ISPs in Vietnam. See http://www.vnnic.net.vn. Regarding regulatory reform of the telecommunications industries in Vietnam, see European Union's Asia IT&C Programme (2004) and International Telecommunication Union (2002).

The cheapest one a college student could purchase cost about US$600. Since GDP per capita in Vietnam was about US$700 in 2005, those who could afford to purchase a new PC were few. Students owning PCs had usually purchased a second-hand PC for about US$150. Most college students had a PC,[10] according to our interviews, though the penetration rate of the Internet in Vietnam, including users at Internet cafes, was 6.55% in 2004. To summarize, the bandwidth of networks was narrow in spite of DSL; Internet access fees were very high; and a PC was expensive compared to Vietnamese income levels.

Most people could not afford to purchase PCs and subscribe to ISPs. In the case of online games, since the hardware prices of computer games matched those in developed countries, children could not afford to buy them. Instead, they played online games at the Internet cafes found on the main street of every town. In particular, in the rural areas, Internet cafes were haunts for children.

In contrast, Internet cafes in HCMC were used for gathering information, e-mailing, making documents, and so on. There were users playing online games, but the percentage was much lower than in rural areas.[11] According to students we interviewed, some college students[12] used Internet cafes to save money instead of subscribing to ISPs. Only a few of the PCs at an Internet cafe I visited in HCMC had a CD-R driver or a USB port. PCs with such functions were positioned in front of a counter at shops to watch what users did. According to the manager of an Internet cafe, few people were using P2P file-sharing. Moreover, according to college students, most users did not know how to use it. That is, P2P file-sharing was seldom utilized at Internet cafes and not familiar to Internet users. This fact could be expected from the speed of networks at Internet cafes. Certainly, in spite of the narrow bandwidth provided by dial-up access, millions of subscribers in the USA used P2P to obtain content. However, subscriptions in the USA have long had

---

[10] Some can obtain portable hard disc players, popular in developed countries, which have promoted file-sharing based on the MP3 format. However, only the wealthy can afford to buy them due to the relatively high cost.

[11] At resorts, as in HCMC, many tourists used Internet cafes.

[12] College students also can access the Internet at computer laboratories within the university. Large universities have such laboratories, but small ones do not. Moreover, students must pay for university use as they do at Internet cafes.

fixed monthly rates. If the fee was dependent on the time of access, the merit of P2P file-sharing would drastically decrease. This was the situation in Vietnam.

2.5 EFFECTS OF ALMOST NON-EXISTENT COPYRIGHT PROTECTION ON FILE-SHARING

In developed countries, copyright has been strictly protected, and the threat of apprehension is credible. Since developed countries have never experienced a situation in the Internet age in which copyright enforcement was largely unworkable due to ineffective measures by the authorities, it is very difficult for researchers in developed countries to consider what would take place in such a situation.

My field research in Vietnam shows that two of the three factors mentioned above, risk of apprehension and low quality, did not seriously influence the use of P2P file-sharing. The first factor did not exist, since the authorities did not implement effective measures to prevent pirated CDs. In such a situation, Internet users were unconcerned about infringement. The second factor apparently did not seriously deter users, since most usually purchased pirated CDs. These facts had positive effects on the spread of P2P file-sharing. Nevertheless, in our interviews, we found that most people did not even know of the existence of P2P file-sharing. This indicates there was little merit for them to use it. Two types of reasons, technical and institutional, explain this situation.

The first of the technical reasons is Internet network speed. As mentioned above, downloading time, dependent on speed, is very important for P2P file-sharing, due to its opportunity costs. Even though content is free, people are not willing to download when the time it takes is lengthy. Therefore, a broadband network or a fixed usage fee is necessary. The second technical reason is the PC price level compared to income. If a PC's price was several times as high as average monthly income, most people could not afford to buy one. The third technical reason is that subscription fees for ISPs were as prohibitive as PC costs. As a result, even if people could obtain free content by P2P file-sharing, transaction costs were higher than the benefits. The primary institutional reason limiting file-sharing is that the pirated-content market had widely penetrated Vietnamese life. In developed countries, P2P file-sharing competes with a legal content market, whereas it competes with a

22   K. DOMON

pirated-content market in Vietnam. Therefore, the advantages of P2P file-sharing in Vietnam were fewer than those in developed countries.

2.6   MEANINGS OF CD SALES FOR SINGERS

Next, I consider the influence of ineffective copyright enforcement on incentives for musicians to produce CDs. In my research, it turned out that, under ineffective copyright enforcement, most singers could not recover the expenses[13] associated with releasing CDs. The main reason for releases was promotion of songs through pirated CDs.

According to a manager, there were three groups among professional singers: the top class earned about US$1000 per 30-minute performance of 6 songs. There were about 20 singers in this group. The second class earned about US$600 per 30-minute performance of 6 songs. About 100 singers belonged to this class. The third class earned about US$200 per 15-minute performance of 3 songs.[14] There were a considerable number of singers in this class.

Vietnamese singers earned money basically from live performances. Their fees reflected how large an audience they could gather. In such a situation, they wanted to advertise their songs, using any method. Due to lack of experience with strict copyright enforcement, most did not realize that (with enforcement) they could earn enough royalties from CD sales to recoup production expenses, so they used pirated CDs as promotional tools. There was a huge difference in the role of CD sales between strictly copyright-protected countries and Vietnam.

Considering the effects of pirated CDs, Vietnamese musicians faced a dilemma between revenues from legal CDs and performance fees. This is explained in Fig. 2.1. The second quadrant shows the relationship between profits from CD sales and the level of copyright enforcement. However, since pirated CDs play a role in promotion, strict copyright enforcement results in a decrease in promotion. This phenomenon is indicated in the third quadrant. Popularity, partly influenced by pirated

---

[13] According to an interview, the cost of a first release of 1000 CDs is at least US$5000. Thus, the CD price must be US$5 to recover cost. However, the price of a copyrighted CD is about US$2.13. If pirated CDs are 90% of total sales, then the first release supplies 9000 pirated CDs for the marketplace at a lesser price.

[14] Most performances in Vietnam included several singers.

2 UNAUTHORIZED COPYING AND INCENTIVES FOR MUSICIANS

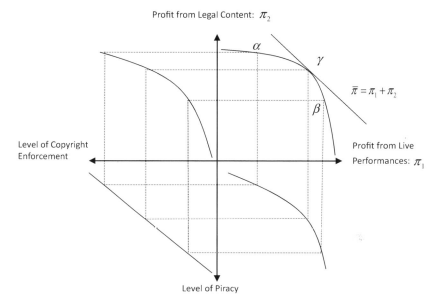

Fig. 2.1 A dilemma of musicians

CDs, determines performance fees on the stage. This relationship is indicated in the fourth quadrant. Finally, we can see the trade-off faced by singers in the first quadrant. Strict copyright enforcement does not assure a beneficial situation for them.[15] In the figure, a decreasing marginal profit with respect to enforcement and piracy promotion, and a negative linear relationship between enforcement and piracy promotion have been assumed. Under these assumptions, as depicted in the first quadrant, the revenue possibility curve is strictly concave.

The specifics of the situation seem to depend on the popularity of the musician. Top musicians, who are already known to and followed by the public, require less promotion of their activities than unknown musicians. The profit possibility curve of such musicians is likely to be steep, so that a profit maximizing point is a corner solution at the vertical axis. Unknown musicians are likely to have a corner solution at the horizontal

---

[15] A similar phenomenon is pointed out in terms of P2P file-sharing. That is, illegal content exchanged by P2P file-sharing contributes to sales of legal CDs.

24   K. DOMON

axis, preferring no copyright enforcement. This is consistent with the result of Mortimer et al. (2012) considering a case in the USA.

2.7   A Model of the Musician's Dilemma

In order to consider the musician's dilemma more carefully, I have created a model. I consider a market in which a copyright holder (a musician)[16] competes with pirates. A musician has two profit sources, live performance and CD sales. Profits from a live performance and a CD sale positively affect each other, since people can come to know singers through either of them.

I assume that a singer is a monopolist in the original CD and performance markets,[17] while a pirate faces perfect competition in the pirated CD market. To simplify notations, a pirate is a representative firm[18] whose production level stands for the market supply of pirated CDs. Since a pirate must obtain an original CD to produce a pirated one, the timing of this game is as follows: a singer first determines q_1 and q_2, and then, a pirate determines q_3.

The profit function of a singer is

$$\pi = \pi_1 + \pi_2 = \{p_1(q_1, q_2, q_3)q_1 - C_1(q_1)\} \\ + \{p_2(q_1, q_2, q_3)q_2 - C_2(q_2)\} \tag{2.1}$$

where π_1 and π_2 are profits, respectively, from the performance and original CD sales. p_1, q_1, and C_1 are, respectively, price, quantity, and a cost function of live performances. p_2, q_2, and C_2 are, respectively, price, quantity, and a cost function of original CDs. q_3 is the quantity of pirated CDs. We need assumptions for the maximum of a profit function. π is strictly concave in q_1 and q_2. C_1 and C_2 are strictly convex. Concerning external effects, I assume $\partial p_1/\partial q_2 > 0$, $\partial p_1/\partial q_3 > 0$, $\partial p_2/\partial q_1 > 0$, and

---

[16] Unlike developed countries, most singers in Vietnam manage to release CDs by themselves. Copyright is held not by recording companies but by the singers themselves. A contract between a singer and a composer utilizes a lump sum paid before releasing a CD.

[17] Substitutability caused by a price change in CDs is smaller than that in other goods, for example, between coffee and tea. When people buy CDs of their favourite singers, they are not likely to buy a CD of another singer when the price of their favourite CD is high. Their decision is only whether to buy or not.

[18] Even if we assume n firms to express perfect competition, results derived in such a situation are the same as those under a representative firm.

$\partial p_2/\partial q_3 < 0$. Due to common price taker behaviour, a pirate's profit function is

$$\Pi = p_3(q_1, q_2)q_3 - C_3(q_3, E), \tag{2.2}$$

where p_3 and C_3 are, respectively, price and a cost function of illegal CDs, and E specifies the level of copyright enforcement. We assume that C_3 is strictly convex with respect to q_3, $\partial p_3/\partial q_1 > 0$, $\partial p_3/\partial q_2 < 0$, $\partial C_3/\partial E > 0$, and $\partial^2 C_3/\partial q_3 \partial E > 0$.

To solve this game, we first obtain the best response of a pirate to the original producer's strategies. The first-order condition for maximizing Π given q_1 and q_2 is,

$$p_3(q_1, q_2) = \frac{\partial C_3(q_3, E)}{\partial q_3}. \tag{2.3}$$

We denote the best response as $\tilde{q}_3(q_1, q_2, E)$, and that $\partial \tilde{q}_3/\partial E < 0$ is apparent.[19] Taking into account this response, a singer maximizes the following function,

$$\tilde{\pi} = \{p_1(q_1, q_2, \tilde{q}_3(q_1, q_2, E))q_1 - C_1(q_1)\} \\ + \{p_2(q_1, q_2, \tilde{q}_3(q_1, q_2, E))q_2 - C_2(q_2)\}. \tag{2.4}$$

A solution for this maximizing problem is denoted as $q_1^*(E)$ and $q_2^*(E)$, and $\tilde{q}_3(q_1, q_2, E)$ finally becomes $\tilde{q}_3^*(q_1^*, q_2^*, E)$. We denote a singer's profit at this equilibrium as

$$\tilde{\pi}^* = \tilde{\pi}_1^* + \tilde{\pi}_2^* = \{p_1^*(q_1^*, q_2^*, \tilde{q}_3^*)q_1^* - C_1(q_1^*)\} \\ + \{p_2^*(q_1^*, q_2^*, \tilde{q}_3^*)q_2^* - C_2(q_2^*)\}. \tag{2.5}$$

We check the impact of E on the sub-game Nash equilibrium in order to consider optimal copyright enforcement for a singer. By total differential of the first-order conditions for profit maximization, we obtain

$$|D| \begin{vmatrix} dq_1 \\ dq_2 \end{vmatrix} = \begin{vmatrix} -\dfrac{\partial^2 \tilde{\pi}}{\partial q_1 \partial E} dE \\ -\dfrac{\partial^2 \tilde{\pi}}{\partial q_2 \partial E} dE \end{vmatrix}, \quad |D| \equiv \begin{vmatrix} \dfrac{\partial^2 \tilde{\pi}}{\partial q_1^2} & \dfrac{\partial^2 \tilde{\pi}}{\partial q_1 \partial q_2} \\ \dfrac{\partial^2 \tilde{\pi}}{\partial q_2 \partial q_1} & \dfrac{\partial^2 \tilde{\pi}}{\partial q_2^2} \end{vmatrix}, \tag{2.6}$$

---

[19] By total differentiation of (2.3) and assumptions regarding C_3, we can obtain this result.

26 K. DOMON

where $|D| > 0$ from the second-order condition for maximization. Therefore, at the equilibrium,

$$\frac{dq_1^*}{dE} = \frac{1}{|D|} \left\{ -\frac{\partial^2 \tilde{\pi}}{\partial q_1 \partial E} \frac{\partial^2 \tilde{\pi}}{\partial q_2^2} + \frac{\partial^2 \tilde{\pi}}{\partial q_1 \partial q_2} \frac{\partial^2 \tilde{\pi}}{\partial q_2 \partial E} \right\}, \tag{2.7}$$

$$\frac{dq_2^*}{dE} = \frac{1}{|D|} \left\{ -\frac{\partial^2 \tilde{\pi}}{\partial q_2 \partial E} \frac{\partial^2 \tilde{\pi}}{\partial q_1^2} + \frac{\partial^2 \tilde{\pi}}{\partial q_2 \partial q_1} \frac{\partial^2 \tilde{\pi}}{\partial q_1 \partial E} \right\}. \tag{2.8}$$

In a country like Vietnam, where live performance is the main source of profits for most musicians, strict enforcement results in a decrease in live performances due to weaker promotion effects from pirated CDs, while still increasing original CD sales. That is, $dq_1^*(E)/dE < 0$ and $dq_2^*(E)/dE > 0$. A necessary and sufficient condition for both inequalities is,

$$\frac{\frac{\partial^2 \tilde{\pi}}{\partial q_2 \partial E} \frac{\partial^2 \tilde{\pi}}{\partial q_1^2}}{\frac{\partial^2 \tilde{\pi}}{\partial q_1 \partial E}} < \frac{\partial^2 \tilde{\pi}}{\partial q_1 \partial q_2} \left(= \frac{\partial^2 \tilde{\pi}}{\partial q_2 \partial q_1} \right) < \frac{\frac{\partial^2 \tilde{\pi}}{\partial q_1 \partial E} \frac{\partial^2 \tilde{\pi}}{\partial q_2^2}}{\frac{\partial^2 \tilde{\pi}}{\partial q_2 \partial E}} \tag{2.9}$$

Proposition 2.1 *Assuming the condition (2.9), a musician's profit strictly increases (or decreases) with the level of copyright enforcement if and only if the marginal promotion effect of pirated CDs, $\partial \pi_1^* / \partial \tilde{q}_3^*$, is smaller (or greater) than the marginal competitive effect of original CDs, $\partial \pi_2^* / \partial \tilde{q}_3^*$.*

From the first-order conditions,

Proof

$$\frac{d\tilde{\pi}^*}{dE} = \frac{\partial \tilde{\pi}^*}{\partial q_1^*} \frac{dq_1^*}{dE} + \frac{\partial \tilde{\pi}^*}{\partial q_2^*} \frac{dq_2^*}{dE} + \frac{\partial \tilde{\pi}^*}{\partial \tilde{q}_3^*} \left(\frac{\partial \tilde{q}_3^*}{\partial E} + \frac{\partial \tilde{q}_3^*}{\partial q_1^*} \frac{dq_1^*}{dE} + \frac{\partial \tilde{q}_3^*}{\partial q_2^*} \frac{dq_2^*}{dE} \right)$$

$$= \left(\frac{\partial \tilde{\pi}_1^*}{\partial \tilde{q}_3^*} + \frac{\partial \tilde{\pi}_2^*}{\partial \tilde{q}_3^*} \right) \left(\underbrace{\frac{\partial \tilde{q}_3^*}{\partial E}}_{-} + \underbrace{\frac{\partial \tilde{q}_3^*}{\partial q_1^*}}_{-} \underbrace{\frac{dq_1^*}{dE}}_{+} + \underbrace{\frac{\partial \tilde{q}_3^*}{\partial q_2^*}}_{-} \underbrace{\frac{dq_2^*}{dE}}_{+} \right).$$

As a result, we obtain this proposition. □

This proposition indicates that pirated CDs are beneficial for a musician when the marginal promotion effect from them is relatively high. A condition for maximizing a singer's profit is $\partial \tilde{\pi}_1^* / \partial \tilde{q}_3^* = -\partial \tilde{\pi}_2^* / \partial \tilde{q}_3^*$.

Figure 2.1 shows three points: γ, at which the maximal profit level is $\bar{\pi}$, α, and β. At α, more piracy increases musician's profits through a promotion effect, even though profits from CDs decrease by lower enforcement. At β, stricter enforcement makes musician's profits higher through an increase in profits from original CD sales, even though profits from live performance decrease with less promotion effect from pirated CDs. In this example, a musician's attitude towards enforcement depends upon the existing enforcement level and the musician's profit function. Top musicians always prefer stricter enforcement, and unknown musicians prefer no enforcement.

2.8 Rational Media Selection by Consumers

In order to consider a concrete situation of P2P file-sharing, in 2006 I collected about 100 samples from college students in Japan, Vietnam, South Korea, and China, and performed interviews with some of them. The interviews and survey data show the differing characteristics of each country regarding use of P2P file-sharing and a common phenomenon regarding purchase of original CDs.

Figure 2.2 shows content acquisition methods in each country. The share of P2P file-sharing in Vietnam was about 9%, while that in South Korea and China was around 70%. In Japan, the share was about 15%. Contrary to interviews and market research, the Vietnamese share was higher than expected. Since most college students in Vietnam belonged to families of the upper middle class or above, it is conceivable that field research in Internet cafes and CD shops, attempting to cover demand for ordinary consumers, was biased.

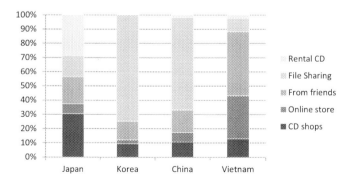

Fig. 2.2 Content acquisition method (multiple answers)

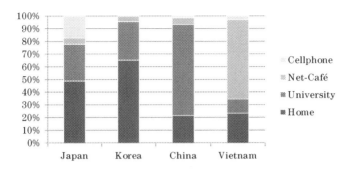

Fig. 2.3 Main location for Internet use (multiple answers)

In viewing this figure, we should also consider the general enforcement levels of illegal products in the four countries. According to the International Intellectual Property Alliance (IIPA),[20] the piracy rates of music content, except for P2P file-sharing, in China, Vietnam, and South Korea, were, respectively, 85, 95, and 7% at that time. In Japan, pirated music CDs and DVDs were impossible for ordinary consumers to access due to strict enforcement and scarce existence in the marketplace. Another important fact is that consumers in China and Vietnam did not discriminate between original and pirated CD shops, since most CD shops there dealt with both CD types under almost no enforcement. The same phenomenon also appeared on the Internet. There were many online stores dealing in illegal music content. In particular, in Vietnam, there were no legal online stores like i-Tunes, and most illegal websites seemed to be making profits from advertisements. An interesting difference between Japan and other countries is the existence of legal rental CD shops, which are permitted by Japanese copyright laws.

In these data, most college students in South Korea and China utilized P2P file-sharing. The percentage was astonishing compared to that of Japan, where at that time P2P file-sharing had become a social issue. To understand the reasons for these differing phenomena, we need more information surrounding college students' lives.

Figure 2.3 shows the main locations for Internet use. In China, most college students lived in dormitories on campus. The situation is reflected in these data. In Vietnam, because the subscriber's fee for an

---

[20] See IIPA Special 301 Letter to USTR, February 12, 2007.

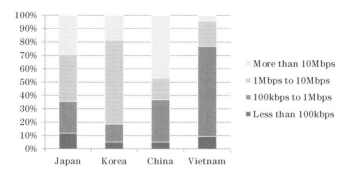

Fig. 2.4 Internet access speed

ISP was expensive compared to income, most students did not have Internet access at home and used Internet cafes and the university. Japan and South Korea have similar ratios, but, since the smartphone had not emerged at that time, though a Japanese cell phone could access the Internet and download music files for listening, cell phones in other countries could not do that.

Along with location data, Internet access speed data characterize each country's situation. Figure 2.4 shows these data. Vietnam's data clearly indicate low access speed, which is explained by location data indicating significant use of Internet cafes, as well as university access at low speeds. In China, according to interviews, college students used high-speed LANs in the dormitory, sharing all kinds of digital content. That is why China's access speed was higher than Japan's and South Korea's. In those days, ADSL had become available nationwide, and also FTTH had begun service in Japan and South Korea. As a result, it turns out that only Vietnam had difficulty using P2P file-sharing because of access speed.

As I explained in Sections 2.4 and 2.5, P2P file-sharing was unpopular in Vietnam, where college students usually bought illegal CDs instead, sharing them among friends (see Fig. 2.2). How many original and illegal CDs and DVDs were purchased in each country is shown in Figs. 2.5 and 2.6. The figures indicate that while the numbers of original CDs and DVDs in Vietnam were similar to numbers in other countries, numbers of illegal CDs and DVDs were much higher than in other countries. This suggests that, in any country, consumers are inclined to buy original CDs of favourite musicians, but that Vietnamese substitute for original CDs of common musicians with illegal CDs.

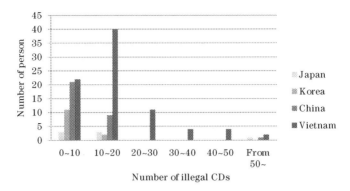

Fig. 2.5 Frequency distribution of number of illegal CDs

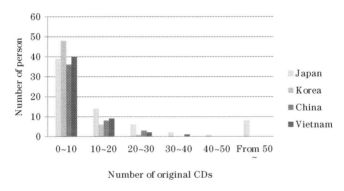

Fig. 2.6 Frequency distribution of number of original CDs

Music content, unlike physical products, can be distributed through many media. This situation is theoretically the same as that in an intermodal competition[21] of the transport industry where travellers can select among modes of movement. Which media consumers select depends upon vertical and horizontal product differentiation and transaction costs, including the risk of apprehension. Demand for each mode or medium depends upon evaluation by consumers.

---

[21] This discussion is also related to deregulation of utility industries and price regulation.

In order to explain the difference in demand for P2P file-sharing in each country, we set up a Cobb–Douglas utility function as follows:

$$U = \prod_{i=1}^{5} q_i^{\alpha_i} \qquad (2.10)$$

where the exponent $\alpha_i > 0$, and q_i is the quantity of product i. There are five kinds of product, an original CD (product 1), a rental original CD (product 2), a music file bought from an online store (product 3), a pirated CD (product 4), and a music file obtained from P2P file-sharing (product 5). The budget constraint is

$$y = \sum_{i=1}^{5} P_i\, q_i, \qquad (2.11)$$

where P_i is the actual cost to obtain a product, including a transaction cost as follows:

$$P_i = p_i + \beta_i \text{ for } i = 1, 2, 3, 4, \text{ and } P_5 = \beta_5, \qquad (2.12)$$

where β_i $(i = 1, \ldots, 5)$ is the transaction cost, including the risk of apprehension when the product is illegal as well as the opportunity cost, and p_i $(i = 1, \ldots, 4)$ is the product price.

The solution maximizing utility under the budget constraint is,

$$q_i^* = \frac{y}{P_i} \times \frac{\alpha_i}{\sum_{j=1}^{5} \alpha_j}. \qquad (2.13)$$

The following proposition is directly derived from this optimal demand equation.

Proposition 2.2 $q_i^* > q_j^* \Leftrightarrow \alpha_i/\alpha_j > P_i/P_j \text{ for } i \neq j \text{ and } i, j = 1, \ldots, 5.$

This suggests that the ratio of preferences and prices determines which demand is greater. In our definition, the price includes a transaction cost that varies by consumer and country.

Focusing on Vietnam's case, in which pirated CDs prevailed over P2P file-sharing, we obtain the following condition,

$$q_4^* > q_5^* \Leftrightarrow p_4 < \frac{\alpha_4}{\alpha_5}\beta_5 - \beta_4. \qquad (2.14)$$

The utility function for most college students in Vietnam satisfied this condition. As explained in Section 2.5, under almost no copyright enforcement, the transaction cost for P2P file-sharing, β_5, was higher than that for an illegal CD for most consumers. However, for wealthy consumers subscribing to an ISP at home, the opportunity cost to obtain an illegal CD may be higher than that of P2P file-sharing, since they must spend time to go shopping. As to α_4 and α_5 representing preference for a product, a great difference between them is not plausible because both products are illegal content of similar quality.

2.9   Concluding Remarks

Methods of listening to music have changed with the invention and evolution of copy technologies. Before copy technologies emerged, professional musicians were usually hired by courts to perform for small audiences of nobles. In the nineteenth century, a new place to play music emerged, i.e. concert halls, where large audiences of the rich listened to music. Until that time, music was always experienced through live performance. Edison's invention of the phonograph drastically changed the music industry, releasing it from the limitations of live performance and increasing the ordinary audience. Even though copying music became possible with this technology, widespread personal copying did not arrive until the compact cassette tape recorder was invented in the 1960s.[22]

In the 1980s, personal copying using compact cassette tape players became commonplace and policymakers discussed royalties related to copyright in developed countries. For example, in Japan, a new law applying levies to an entire medium was created in order for copyright holders to retrieve royalties lost to personal copying. In the same period, developing countries were full of illegal copies. In the twentieth century, developed and developing countries experienced different situations regarding illegal music copying, but currently, musicians in both types of country seem to be returning to live performance to make profits, since free music on the Internet and smartphones prevails around the world due to the drastic reduction in transaction costs for delivering music files.

In this chapter, I have considered incentives for musicians to release CDs and media selection by consumers. Nowadays, music content on the

---

[22]See Kimizuka (2012).

Internet in developed countries is largely treated as promotion to recruit fans and attract them to live concerts. My research has found that this phenomenon has existed in developing countries with no enforcement of copyright since personal copying was invented, and that a great deal of music content has been supplied for this purpose. Copyright should be considered differently for each product. The above considerations are not applicable to, for example, copyright of books. An important factor which makes music content different from books is the range of revenue sources. A book author's live performance generally only produces profits from the books purchased to be signed. Regarding the medium selected for listening to music, I have explained from sample data that not only price, but also transaction cost influences the selection. The transaction cost includes various factors, and the level of enforcement is one of them. In the Internet era, most people on the globe can easily access and obtain information by PC and smartphone, and that makes transaction costs extremely low. P2P file-sharing was a disruptive phenomenon we faced at the end of the twentieth century. What constitutes effective copyright has changed, and industries must adjust their businesses by taking into account listeners' rational media selection.

REFERENCES

Andersen, B., & Frenz, M. (2010). Don't Blame the P2P File-Sharers: The Impact of Free Music Downloads on the Purchase of Music CDs in Canada. *Journal of Evolutionary Economics, 20*(5), 715–740.

Barker, G., & Maloney, T. (2015). The Impact of Internet File-Sharing on the Purchase of Music CDs in Canada. *Journal of Evolutionary Economics, 25*(4), 821–848.

Besen, S. M., & Kirby, S. N. (1989). Private Copying, Appropriability, and Optimal Copying Royalties. *Journal of Law and Economics, 32*(2), 255–280.

Domon, K. (2006). Price Discrimination of Digital Content. *Economics Letters, 93*(3), 421–426.

Domon, K., & Lam, T. D. (2009). Profitable Piracy in Music Industries. *Review of Economic Research on Copyright Issues, 6*(1), 1–11.

Domon, K., & Nakamura, K. (2007). Unauthorized Copying and Copyright Enforcement in Developing Countries: A Vietnam Case Study. *Review of Economic Research on Copyright Issues, 4*(1), 87–96.

Domon, K., & Yamazaki, N. (2004). Unauthorized File-Sharing and the Pricing of Digital Content. *Economics Letters, 85*(2), 179–184.

European Union's Asia IT&C Programme. (2004). *Promoting Internet Policy and Regulatory Reform in Vietnam: Status of Telecommunications Development in Vietnam.*

Gordon, W. J. (1982). Fair Use as Market Failure: A Structural and Economic Analysis of the Betamax Case and Its Predecessors. *Columbia Law Review, 82,* 1600–1657.

International Telecommunication Union. (2002). *Vietnam Internet Case Study.* Geneva.

Kimizuka, M. (2012). Historical Development of Magnetic Recording and Tape Recorder. *Gijutsu no Keitouka Chousa Houkokusho* (in Japanese) 17. Center of the History of Japanese Industrial Technology.

Liebowitz, S. J. (1985). Copying and Indirect Appropriability: Photocopying of Journals. *Journal of Political Economy, 93*(5), 945–957.

Liebowitz, S. J. (2016). How Much of the Decline in Sound Recording Sales Is Due to File-Sharing? *Journal of Cultural Economics, 40,* 13–28.

Mortimer, J. M., Nosko, C., & Sorensen, M. (2012). Supply Responses to Digital Distribution: Recorded Music and Live Performances. *Information Economics and Policy, 24*(1), 3–14.

Varian, H. R. (2000). Buying, Sharing and Renting Information Goods. *Journal of Industrial Economics, 48*(4), 473–488.

Varian, H. R. (2005). Copying and Copyright. *Journal of Economic Perspectives, 19*(2), 121–138.

CHAPTER 3

Fake Spare Parts When No Domestic Brand Names Can Be Trusted

Abstract This chapter considers fake motorcycle spare parts whose value is determined by duration and quality. A bad image about domestic products, which is often present in developing countries, causes consumers to distrust domestic brand names. That is a major reason why fake packaging was pervasive in Vietnam. I first explain the fact, obtained by field research, that repairpersons have incentives not only to use fake spare parts but also to mitigate incomplete consumer information about quality. I then analyse this phenomenon in a theoretical model, indicating inconsistent incentives concerning social welfare and consumers' surpluses. I also consider a counterfeiting game between counterfeiters producing products of differing quality and show that a counterfeiter producing second-tier products does not always prefer no enforcement, while a counterfeiter producing lowest quality products always prefers it.

Keywords Counterfeiting game · Fake spare parts · Incomplete information

3.1 BACKGROUND

Most Asian nations are still emerging and developing, dependent upon technologies created by developed countries. To catch up and then compete with developed countries, they must invest in R&D and produce

© The Author(s) 2018
K. Domon, *An Economic Analysis of Intellectual Property Rights Infringement*, Palgrave Studies in Institutions, Economics and Law,
https://doi.org/10.1007/978-3-319-90466-5_3

their own brand names. However, as seen in China, steps in this process are sometimes skipped, legally through joint ventures and illegally by violating IP laws.[1]

I investigated the spare parts market for motorcycles in Vietnam, Cambodia, Laos, the Philippines, and Indonesia. Motorcycles are the most popular form of transport in these countries, due to a lack of public transportation. Observing phenomena there, revealing how producers, retailers, and consumers react to a situation without reliable information concerning product quality allowed us to consider how incentives can be compatible between developing and developed countries, providing bases for working together to create structures for strict trademark enforcement.

Before proceeding, I will provide a brief history of the motorcycle market in Vietnam.[2] The first motorcycle imported in quantity to Vietnam was the Honda Super Cab, in the 1960s. This model is still popular in Asia due to its high durability. After the Vietnam War, Vietnam closed its market to western countries and strove to build a centralized economy. During this period, second-hand motorcycles, those surviving the Vietnam War and newly imported ones from Eastern Europe, were traded in the market. After the failure of the centralized economy, Vietnam opened its market and introduced a partly free market, called "Doi Moi", as China had done. This market reform was successful, and people with high incomes could afford to buy motorcycles. In the 1990s, the Vietnamese government implemented an import-substitution policy in order to foster domestic industries. Japanese and Taiwanese companies began to invest and produce motorcycles in Vietnam by assembling imported parts (and, later, domestic parts) under a new regulation. In 2000, Chinese companies targeted the Vietnamese market for the sale of parts and of whole kits overproduced in China,[3]

---

[1] In China, local governments must entangle themselves with counterfeiting in order to protect economies to some extent dependent upon such activities. These governments also obtain taxes from counterfeiters. See Chow (2010) regarding the importance of the counterfeiting business in China.

[2] The explanation follows Fujita (2007, 2008). There are few papers and reports available regarding the motorcycle industry in Vietnam.

[3] At the turn of the millennium, counterfeit motorcycles and parts were often produced in China. The technique of producing such products was remarkable. Hung (2003) describes the case of Yamaha motorcycles.

and new domestic assemblers emerged and supplied cheap motorcycles in Vietnam. Since there were many people who could not afford to buy expensive Japanese and Taiwanese motorcycles, Chinese models instantly claimed a large market share. However, since people recognized low quality in the Chinese models, as competitors arose to supply cheap motorcycles to ordinary people, the Chinese share gradually dropped. Nowadays, people prefer brand-name motorcycles of high quality and can afford to buy them due to increasing incomes. Chinese motorcycles have almost disappeared and survive only in rural areas and for the poor.

Now, there are many kinds of spare parts, of varying quality, in Vietnam. The best are imported from Japan. The second best are produced by Japanese and Taiwanese companies in Vietnam, and next are spare parts imported from Thailand, from which Japanese and Taiwanese parts makers supply assemblers in Asia. The lowest quality parts are imported from China. There are also small and medium-sized Vietnamese companies that supply foreign assemblers, but detailed information about them cannot be obtained because few official statistics exist. It is important for our discussions that many kinds of spare parts, including smuggled parts, are available in the marketplace.

A number of references[4] provide context for this work. This chapter's considerations directly relate to several discussions on counterfeiting. First is that of credence goods, defined by Darby and Karni (1973), describing products whose quality is difficult for consumers to distinguish even after using them. A repair service offers a typical example of such goods. Under asymmetric information, a mechanic can find a broken part to fix while a customer cannot. Fraud by a mechanic in an automobile repair shop is a common phenomenon. Selling counterfeit spare parts seems a similar problem, but over the long term customers can generally distinguish the quality of the parts. Therefore, counterfeits

---

[4]Papers directly related to counterfeiting in this market have increased since around 2000, according to Staake et al. (2009). The period coincides with the rapid economic development of Asian countries, especially China. Counterfeits made in China have certainly influenced this trend. Since counterfeiting issues have practical effects on actual businesses, a number of papers approach this problem from a marketing and business perspective. Kaikati and LaGarce (1980) suggest comprehensive remedies for counterfeiting in developing countries. Through interviews, Minagawa et al. (2007) consider technology acquisition by reverse engineering, with resultant counterfeit products and patent law infringement, in China. Olsen and Granzin (1993) focus on distribution channels to combat counterfeiting in US automobile markets.

38   K. DOMON

themselves are not credence goods, but advice or recommendations by mechanics represent credence services. Dulleck and Kerschbamer (2006) have classified and summarized discussions about expert advice as a credence service.

Few papers in economics consider actual situations of trademark[5] infringement taking place in developing and emerging countries. Grossman and Shapiro (1988a, b) consider counterfeiting in a theoretical model where counterfeit products are imported from abroad to developed countries. Their focus differs from the focus here, which considers domestic problems of counterfeiting within developing countries. Because of rapid economic growth in emerging and developing countries, this chapter focuses on the competition between counterfeit and genuine products within developing countries. Higgins and Rubin (1986) consider snob effects on counterfeiting in a luxury product market, taking enforcement into account. In the spare parts markets considered in this paper, there are also such effects, and quality is an important factor in making the decision to purchase.

The treatment proceeds as follows. First, after explaining the characteristics of counterfeits considered in this section, I show how consumers react to incomplete information on product quality. Second, I show incentives for wholesalers and retailers to reveal real quality information to consumers, taking into account the market structure. Third, I consider how a bad image of domestic products affects market performance by using a model and show that strict law enforcement does not increase social welfare in a developing country like Vietnam. Fourth, I consider the incentives of producers to demand strict enforcement, indicating that counterfeiters need strictness when they produce relatively high-quality goods; however, Nash equilibrium between middle- and low-quality producers under no enforcement produces an incentive to counterfeit. Finally, I summarize the conclusions reached.

3.2   Incomplete Information for Consumers

In Vietnam, there is much trademark infringement with almost no enforcement. In spite of this situation, consumers need information about product quality. According to motorcycle repairpersons in 2011

---

[5] Concerning the role of trademarks in economics, see Ramello (2006).

and 2012,[6] consumers did not buy spare parts with unknown or non-brand packages. Most did not trust non-brand products, especially those made in Vietnam and China. As a result, unknown producers imitated the packaging and logos of well-known brand names. Many consumers, however, could not afford to buy authentic products, especially those made in Japan or by Japanese companies in Vietnam. In such cases, shop owners often recommended counterfeit spare parts suitable for the customer's budget without saying that they were counterfeits.[7] Rather than deceiving consumers simply to earn high margins, they often sold counterfeits as originals but at an appropriate price for the buyer.

We can consider three possible reasons for the phenomenon that consumers were unlikely to buy non-brand-name products even though there were many fake products carrying famous brand names.

First, consumers can perceive a positive signal from a fake package and logo. For consumers, such a signal might suggest that these counterfeiters of authentic spare parts have enough profit to invest in package imitation. Large profits from deceiving consumers would be difficult for repair shops to obtain, because they would lose customers due to loss of reputation, as will be shown later. This would result in lowering the profits of low-quality counterfeiters. In the marketplace, low-quality counterfeits could not make enough profit to invest in imitation, while high-quality counterfeits could afford it. Under incomplete information about quality, this situation is similar to a signalling game that uses a fake package. This scenario would be particularly convincing if original brand-name spare parts producers invented costly anti-imitation packages. And indeed, some producers are struggling to inform consumers of the authenticity of their spare parts by using packaging that is difficult for counterfeiters to imitate.[8] A costly imitation makes profits for high-quality, but not for low-quality, counterfeiters.

---

[6]We performed interviews in eight repair shops and with many dealers in Ho Chi Minh City in December 2011 and July 2012, in Pleiku in December 2011, and in Da Nang in December 2012.

[7]A respondent in a repair shop informed us (December 2011) that, in Ho Chi Minh City's Chinatown, there was a factory, run by Chinese Vietnamese, producing high-quality fake parts. The quality was good, and such parts were recommended to consumers who could not afford to buy genuine Japanese parts due to high prices.

[8]An example of such anti-imitation efforts is a package with a barcode that can be checked online. This system is also used to control spare parts for automobiles. We saw

Second, consumers often obtain quality information from repair shops. Many repair shops tell consumers about actual quality in order to maintain good reputations. In such situations, consumers are willing to buy counterfeit spare parts even knowing they are fake, following advice from repairpersons, and the package and logo are not important. Furthermore, counterfeiters can reduce the cost of packaging by using common packaging. It is said that there are underground networks to produce fake packaging and logos. Since most underground factories use the same brand name, an economy of scale reduces the cost of production. Therefore, counterfeiters obtain benefits from using a common brand name. However, in such a case, signalling alone does not allow consumers to judge the quality of counterfeit spare parts.

The third factor is explained by market structure. There are two separate markets, consisting of temporary and permanent repair shops (Fig. 3.1). The former market is found in the street and often changes its location. Facing trouble in the street or at night, people use such shops, as they do not have another choice. Even when a temporary repair shop sells a recognizable counterfeit as original at a high price, people have no choice to go to another shop, so they buy it. This temporary business is possible because a great number of people use motorcycles. The latter market is comprised of fixed stores in buildings, doing business for the long run. As explained just above, such shops often choose not to deceive consumers. Consumers are mostly deceived in temporary shops, but, lacking other options, cannot avoid the risk of buying counterfeits. Counterfeiters supply spare parts for both markets to make profits. Consumers passively purchase counterfeits with brand names in temporary shops, because using unknown parts carries risk, too.

Unlike the incomplete information possessed by consumers, there is reasonably complete information between wholesalers and repair shops. Wholesalers and repair shops play the key role of intermediary between producers and consumers. Wholesalers buy spare parts directly from producers and are fully informed about quality due to their long business

---

such systems in China, Thailand, and Vietnam. A local city, Kunming, in China, has managed to assure genuine parts by developing commercial districts in which almost all parts are confirmed by barcode, as well as by appointing local officers who always watch dealings (February 2012). However, according to an interview of a motorcycle repairperson in Bangkok, Thailand, fake part producers also imitate this system (July 2012). He said that he can finally check if a part is genuine or fake through his eyes and touch, though when consumers see such a package, they cannot know if it is fake or not.

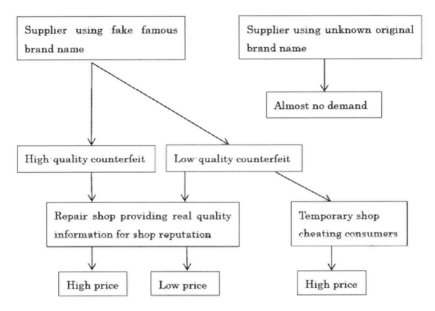

Fig. 3.1 Market for famous fake brand-name products versus original-name domestic products

relationships. Such relationships are also built between wholesalers and repair shops. Except for small sole-proprietor shops, repairpersons obtain quality information from wholesalers.[9] In general, wholesalers and repair shops have accurate knowledge of genuine and counterfeit spare parts. For them, information on spare parts is complete.

3.3 Incomplete Information on Quality of Domestic Products

A Model

In the above section, I explained that a repair shop as an intermediary informed consumers of the real quality of domestic spare parts with fake

---

[9] In interviews, staff at most repair shops reported that wholesalers mark fake parts in order for buyers to distinguish them from genuine parts. Between wholesalers and repair shops, fake parts are considered cheap substitutes for genuine parts. Small shops often purchase from black markets where fake, second-hand, and stolen genuine parts are available. One such market, famous in Ho Chi Minh City, is Tan Thanh Market.

42 K. DOMON

packaging. If the explanation was perfect, market distortion by incomplete information would disappear in spite of fake packaging. This situation is just the same as that with a package with an original brand name. This subsection considers the effects of a general bad image of domestic products on a market.[10] The general bad image creates incomplete information in a market and can partly explain the existence of fake packages.

A model is set up as follows. Consumers are uniformly distributed in $[\underline{v}, \overline{v}]$, and market demand is expressed by length of a line in $[\underline{v}, \overline{v}]$. Consumer i's evaluation of a product is $v_i(\underline{v} \leq v_i \leq \overline{v})$. Her or his utility function is

$$U_i^F = v_i t^F - p^F \tag{3.1}$$

when buying a foreign product, and

$$U_i^D = v_i \lambda t^D - p^D \ (0 < \lambda \leq 1) \tag{3.2}$$

when buying a domestic product. t^F and t^D $(t^F > t^D)$ are respectively quality of a foreign (F) and of a domestic (D) product. p^F and p^D are respectively price of a foreign and of a domestic product. λ expresses the general impression of a domestic product. $\lambda = 1$ suggests complete information on quality. As λ decreases, the impression of quality worsens. Quality information of a foreign product is assumed to be complete, since consumers can buy original foreign products at the official repair shops of makers. Such shops exist not only in big cities, but also in rural areas, except for mountainous regions and small villages.

Note that λ does not express the level of enforcement but the level of bad image. If law enforcement is perfect, consumers buy either a domestic or a foreign original product. In this case—which has never taken place—we can consider two scenarios regarding a relationship between law enforcement and λ:

Scenario I: Soon after perfect enforcement, a bad image disappears $(\lambda = 1)$.

This scenario assumes that consumers understand the real quality of domestic products when they cannot buy a counterfeit. But, until they learn the real quality, they must try to use domestic spare parts (experience goods) with unknown brand names. Therefore, even if a consumer

---

[10]A good image of foreign products may also cause incomplete information on quality. Consumers could overestimate the quality of foreign products. For producers and countries, a good national brand image is beneficial even if low-quality products are made.

could not select a counterfeit, a bad image would not disappear immediately upon perfect enforcement.

Scenario II: Even after perfect enforcement, a bad image persists $(\lambda < 1)$.

This scenario is realistic in the short run. A bad image gradually decreases in the long run, but it takes a long time to erase the image. For a realistic consideration, I adopt Scenario II in this analysis and assume that enforcement moves λ closer to one.

I will consider later the role of repair shops that intermediate between producers and consumers, and first obtain market equilibrium. After considering it, I interpret the role of repair shops in the marketplace. They inform consumers of the real quality of fake domestic spare parts, mitigating incomplete information.

The profit functions of foreign and domestic producers are

$$\pi^F = p^F q^F - t^F q^F, \ \pi_h^D = p^D q_h^D - t^D q_h^D \ (h = 1, 2, \ldots, n). \quad (3.3)$$

A market contains one foreign and many domestic producers. Symmetric domestic producers face an oligopoly competition, and at the Nash equilibrium, price is assumed to be approximately equal to marginal cost. That result is obtained if the number of producers is infinite or the market is very competitive. Therefore, a foreign producer considers $p^D = t^D$ in maximizing profit.[11]

Equilibrium

In order to obtain demand functions for a foreign and a domestic product, a critical consumer satisfying $U_i^F = U_i^D$ must be identified. The consumer's location is

$$\tilde{v} = \frac{p^F - p^D}{t^F - \lambda t^D} \left(\equiv \frac{\Delta p}{\Delta t} \right). \quad (3.4)$$

Demand functions for a foreign and a domestic product are respectively obtained as follows,

$$q^F = \bar{v} - \tilde{v}, \ q^D = \tilde{v} - \underline{v}. \quad (3.5)$$

---

[11]A fringe firm model is also applicable. In the model, a fringe firm determines supply as a price taker. A dominant firm, here an original producer, determines price by considering the fringe firm's supply.

44   K. DOMON

A solution at the market equilibrium is as follows,

$$q^{F*} = \frac{\overline{v}}{2} - \frac{t^F - t^D}{2\Delta t}, \tag{3.6}$$

$$q^{D*} = \frac{p^{F*} - p^{D*}}{\Delta t} - \underline{v} = \frac{1}{2\Delta t}\left\{(\overline{v}+1)t^F - (\lambda\overline{v}+1)t^D\right\} - \underline{v}, \tag{3.7}$$

$$p^{F*} = p^D + (\overline{v} - q^{F*})\Delta t = \frac{1+\overline{v}}{2}t^F + \frac{1-\lambda\overline{v}}{2}t^D. \tag{3.8}$$

Incentives of Producers and Consumers

Two impacts of λ on the equilibrium are considered separately, an impact on domestic social welfare and one on foreign social welfare, where the domestic impact is defined only as consumers' surplus (due to the assumption of zero profit for domestic producers) and the foreign impact is a foreign producer's profit. I consider two kinds of incentive compatibility in λ. One is between a developing and a developed country; the other is between the consumers of domestic and foreign products.

First, it is apparent that a general bad image of domestic products increases profits of a foreign producer. That is, $d\pi^{F*}/d\lambda < 0$.[12] A product with an original domestic brand name is underestimated due to incomplete information regarding quality.

Second, domestic consumers are damaged by incomplete information on quality. Consumers' surplus from foreign and domestic products after consumption are respectively defined as follows,

$$\mathrm{CS}^F = \int_{\tilde{v}}^{\overline{v}} \left(v_i t^F - p^{F*}\right) dv_i = (\overline{v} - \tilde{v})\left\{\frac{1}{2}t^F(\overline{v} + \tilde{v}) - p^{F*}\right\}, \tag{3.9}$$

$$\mathrm{CS}^D = \int_{\underline{v}}^{\tilde{v}} \left(v_i t^D - t^D\right) dv_i = (\tilde{v} - \underline{v})\left\{\frac{1}{2}t^D(\tilde{v} + \underline{v}) - t^D\right\}, \tag{3.10}$$

which are depicted in Fig. 3.2. After use, consumers realize the real quality of domestic products, as they are experience goods. Therefore, the

[12] See Appendix 3.1.

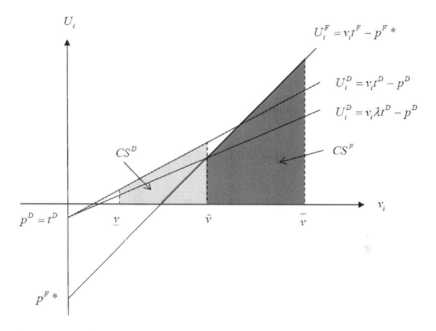

Fig. 3.2 Market equilibrium under experience goods

consumers' surplus stemming from a domestic product is evaluated by real quality after purchase, while equilibrium is determined under incomplete information. This situation causes a market distortion.

Regarding consumers' surpluses, the following proposition is obtained,

Proposition 3.1 $\dfrac{d\mathrm{CS}^F}{d\lambda} \begin{Bmatrix} > \\ = \\ < \end{Bmatrix} 0 \Leftrightarrow -\dfrac{t^F \tilde{v} - p^{F*}}{\overline{v} - \tilde{v}} \begin{Bmatrix} > \\ = \\ < \end{Bmatrix} \dfrac{dp^{F*}/d\lambda}{d\tilde{v}/d\lambda},$

$\dfrac{d\mathrm{CS}^D}{d\lambda} > 0,$ and $\dfrac{d(\mathrm{CS}^F + \mathrm{CS}^D)}{d\lambda} > 0.$

Proof

$$\dfrac{d\mathrm{CS}^F}{d\lambda} = -\underbrace{\left(t^F \tilde{v} - p^{F*}\right)}_{+} \underbrace{\dfrac{d\tilde{v}}{d\lambda}}_{+} - \underbrace{(\overline{v} - \tilde{v})}_{+} \underbrace{\dfrac{dp^{F*}}{d\lambda}}_{-}.$$

46   K. DOMON

$\left(t^F \tilde{v} - \tilde{p}^{F*}\right)$ is strictly positive because it is the utility of a consumer i at $v_i = \tilde{v}$, and $(\bar{v} - \tilde{v})$ is strictly positive. As a result,

$$\frac{dCS^F}{d\lambda} \left\{ \begin{array}{c} > \\ = \\ < \end{array} \right\} 0 \Leftrightarrow -\frac{t^F \tilde{v} - p^{F*}}{\bar{v} - \tilde{v}} \left\{ \begin{array}{c} > \\ = \\ < \end{array} \right\} \frac{dp^{F*}/d\lambda}{d\tilde{v}/d\lambda},$$

and also,

$$\frac{dCS^D}{d\lambda} = \left(t^D \tilde{v} - t^D\right) \cdot \frac{d\tilde{v}}{d\lambda} = \left. v_i \right|_{\substack{v_i = \tilde{v} \\ \lambda = 1}} \cdot \frac{d\tilde{v}}{d\lambda} > 0,$$

Furthermore,

$$\frac{dCS^F}{d\lambda} + \frac{dCS^D}{d\lambda} = \left\{ t^D \underbrace{(\tilde{v} - 1)}_{+} - \underbrace{\left(t^F \tilde{v} - p^{F*}\right)}_{+} \right\} \underbrace{\frac{d\tilde{v}}{d\lambda}}_{+} - \underbrace{(\bar{v} - \tilde{v})}_{+} \underbrace{\frac{dp^{F*}}{d\lambda}}_{-}$$

$$= \underbrace{\left(\left. U_i^D \right|_{\substack{v_i = \tilde{v} \\ \lambda = 1}} - \left. U_i^F \right|_{v_i = \tilde{v}} \right)}_{+} \underbrace{\frac{d\tilde{v}}{d\lambda}}_{+} - \underbrace{(\bar{v} - \tilde{v})}_{+} \underbrace{\frac{dp^{F*}}{d\lambda}}_{-} > 0. \quad \square$$

The first term of $dCS^F/d\lambda$ in the proof indicates a marginal effect of λ on $\tilde{v}$ at equilibrium. Since the number of consumers, $\bar{v} - \tilde{v}$, decreases with λ, this term is strictly negative. In other words, demand for foreign products increases if the level of a bad image increases. The second term indicates a marginal effect of λ on p^{F*} at equilibrium. Since all consumers obtain benefits from a price reduction by competition, this term is strictly positive. In other words, a decrease in λ leads to a price increase, and consumers' surplus goes down. Whether CS^F increases with λ depends upon which term is greater than the other. Some consumers preferring foreign products change to domestic products due to an increase in λ.

Regarding CS^D, due to $p^D = t^D$, $dCS^D/d\lambda$ does not display a marginal effect of λ on p^D at equilibrium. Therefore, $dCS^D/d\lambda$ exhibits only a positive effect of λ on $\tilde{v}$, an increase in consumers buying a domestic product. A decrease in a bad image leads to an increase in CS^D.

Finally, regarding total consumers' surplus, the sign of $d(CS^F + CS^D)/d\lambda$ is strictly positive, meaning that consumers' surplus over the whole market increases with a decrease in a bad image. For consumers as a whole, complete information, $\lambda = 1$, is best. Since domestic producers' surplus is zero, domestic social welfare is also increasing when λ gets closer to one.

Between developing and developed countries, an inconsistency exists regarding incentives about λ. For developing countries, $\lambda = 1$ is best, while for developed countries the smallest λ is best. From this result, we should understand one role of fake packaging.

Proposition 3.2 *A developed country prefers the smallest λ under no enforcement[13] while a developing county prefers the largest $\lambda(=1)$ under perfect enforcement.*

Proof It is obvious from $d\pi^{F*}/d\lambda < 0$ and $d(\mathrm{CS}^F + \mathrm{CS}^D)/d\lambda > 0$. $\square$

A fake package can mitigate incomplete information causing a bad image. If consumers are cheated and buy low-quality products at high prices, domestic social welfare is damaged. However, in an actual market, not all, but most, repair shops explain quality accurately and sell spare parts with fake packages at appropriate prices. This repairers' explanation can make λ closer to one. Reasons why domestic authorities do not enforce strictly fake spare parts seem first that enforcement is costly within limited budgets; second, that an improvement in a general bad image is not easy; and third, that authorities realize the role of repairers in mitigating incomplete information. Therefore, a fake package plays an important role in increasing domestic social welfare. The real problem is not legal infringement, but incomplete or missing information. Merely condemning infringement[14] does not solve the problem.

---

[13] In fact a good image or complete information about the quality of domestic products can trigger a severe competition between domestic and foreign companies, as explained in Section 3.4.

[14] At seminars joined by Japanese motorcycle makers, they complained about counterfeits. In discussions, they express concern about the reputation of their products, since there are fatal accidents caused by fake parts, like a front fork, with their brand names. However, in terms of spare parts, they seem not to mind seriously. In other industries, such as consumer electronics and processed foods, there are foreign companies jointly enforcing counterfeits with local authorities, financially supporting them. But I have not heard that Japanese motorcycle makers engage in such joint enforcement even though they have enough money.

Consumers of foreign and domestic products also have an inconsistency regarding incentives about λ. Proposition 3.1 indicates that consumers preferring a foreign product may lose surpluses, while consumers preferring domestic products increase surpluses, when λ gets closer to one. This conflict between consumers is caused by getting rid of market distortion and is a sound phenomenon as a whole. However, it is ironic that relatively rich consumers who can afford to buy foreign products benefit from incomplete information and market distortion.

3.4 Counterfeiters' Incentives to Create Original Brands

A Model

In the marketplace, we can see many levels of quality in counterfeit spare parts, as explained in the above subsections. In the past, there were producers of counterfeits who tried to sell under original brand names, but in Vietnam, when I did research, most had failed. Such trials suggest that second-tier producers sought to enter the market for original spare parts, but could not profit even with reasonable prices. It seems that they realized higher profitability by counterfeiting than by producing originals and withdrew from the original market.

In the previous subsection, I explained that counterfeiting without cheating consumers is beneficial for domestic producers whose products have a bad image. There is another situation in which cheating consumers is beneficial under competition with other counterfeiters. Cheating of consumers was seen in temporary repair shops, as explained in Fig. 3.1, and sometimes in fixed stores whose staffs often cheated customers not for the shop, but for their personal profit. Although shop owners oversee them, they can move to other shops before their behaviours are detected.[15] Therefore, there is a demand for counterfeits to cheat consumers, and counterfeiters compete with each other to fill this demand.

I analyse this situation by using an oligopoly model in which there are three Firms—L, M, and H—producing, respectively, low-, middle-, and high-quality spare parts and three types of consumers—L, M, and

---

[15] Staff in repair shops steal genuine parts from customers' motorbikes, replacing them with cheap fakes, and sell the genuine items at a black market. This is a common phenomenon, and many customers are careful to prevent such theft.

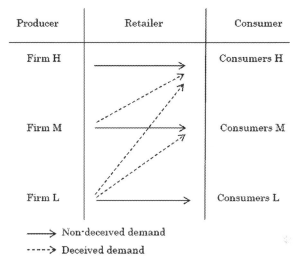

Fig. 3.3 Demand structure of counterfeiting game

H—who demand, respectively, low-, middle-, and high-quality spare parts. In this model, I consider incentives to produce counterfeits and deceive consumers, and show that producers making middle-quality spare parts must counterfeit to compete with counterfeiters making low-quality parts at a Nash equilibrium. I also show the condition that producers making middle-quality spare parts may increase profits under strict enforcement. That is, all counterfeiters do not always prefer lax enforcement.

Figure 3.3 shows a demand structure under no enforcement of trademark laws. Horizontal arrows represent correct demands without cheating consumers, and upward arrows show demands for counterfeits. In complete information, the upward arrows disappear. That is, when a counterfeiter cannot sell products deceptively, she or he loses demand.

Inverse demands in consumers H, M, and L are assumed to be separated as follows,

$$p^H(q^H, q_M^H, q_L^H) = a^H - b^H q^H - b_M^H q_M^H - b_L^H q_L^H, \qquad (3.11)$$

$$p^M(q^M, q_L^M) = a^M - b^M q^M - b_L^M q_L^M, \qquad (3.12)$$

$$p^L(q^L) = a^L - b^L q^L, \qquad (3.13)$$

50 K. DOMON

where p^i and $q^i (i = H, M, L)$ are respectively a price and a non-deceptive demand in a market for consumers i. a^i and b^i are strictly positive parameters and $a^H > a^M > a^L$ is assumed due to a high marginal utility for a high-quality product. q_M^H and q_L^H are the amounts of counterfeits supplied by, respectively, Firms M and L in the high-quality market, and q_L^M is the amount of counterfeits supplied by Firm L in the middle-quality market. The effects of counterfeits on demands are expressed by strictly positive parameters b_M^H, b_L^H, and b_L^M. The costs for producing high-, middle-, and low-quality spare parts are, respectively, c^H, c^M, and c^L ($c^H > c^M > c^L$).

An Equilibrium

A game has three periods. In the first period, Firms M and L determine whether to produce counterfeit spare parts or not. Strategy O is denoted as production of original spare parts and Strategy F as production of counterfeit spare parts. In the second period, Firm H determines the quantity of original spare parts, and then, in the third period, Firms M and L engage in quantity competition.

This game is solved by backward induction. We first obtain a Nash equilibrium in the third period. Profit functions of Firms M and L are

$$\pi^M = p^M q^M + p^H q_M^H - c^M \cdot (q^M + q_M^H), \tag{3.14}$$

$$\pi^L = p^L q^L + p^H q_L^H + p^M q_L^M - c^L \cdot (q^L + q_L^H + q_L^M). \tag{3.15}$$

Given q^H, we can obtain the Nash equilibrium as follows,

$$q^{M*} = \frac{1}{3b^M}(a^M - 2c^M + c^L), \tag{3.16}$$

$$q_M^{H*} = \frac{1}{3b_M^H}(a^H - b^H q^H - 2c^M + c^L), \tag{3.17}$$

$$q_L^{M*} = \frac{1}{3b_L^M}(a^M + c^M - 2c^L), \tag{3.18}$$

$$q_L^{H*} = \frac{1}{3b_L^H}(a^H - b^H q^H + c^M - 2c^L), \tag{3.19}$$

$$q^{L*} = \frac{1}{2b^L}(a^L - c^L). \tag{3.20}$$

Next, we solve the maximization problem of Firm H in the second period, taking into account these solutions. Firm H's profit function is

$$\pi^H = p^H q^H - c^M q^H \tag{3.21}$$

From the first-order condition of this problem, we obtain

$$q^{H**} = \frac{1}{2b^H}(a^H - 3c^H + c^M + c^L), \tag{3.22}$$

and, inserting this into Nash equilibrium in the third period, we obtain

$$q_M^{H**} = \frac{1}{6b_M^H}(a^H + 3c^H - 5c^M + c^L), \tag{3.23}$$

$$q_L^{H**} = \frac{1}{6b_L^H}(a^H + 3c^H + c^M - 5c^L) \tag{3.24}$$

Table 3.1 Counterfeiting game in the first period

		Firm L	
		O	F
Firm M	O	π_{OO}^M, π_{OO}^L	π_{OF}^M, π_{OF}^L
	F	$\underline{\pi_{FO}^M}, \pi_{FO}^L$	$\underline{\pi_{FF}^M}, \underline{\pi_{FF}^L}$

Finally, we consider a counterfeiting game in the first period where Firms M and L make the decision of whether to produce counterfeits or not. In the above sub-game, we solved only the situation of (F, F), indicated in Table 3.1, in the first period. In order to obtain a sub-game Nash equilibrium, we must solve profits in the other three situations. However, the Nash equilibrium in Table 3.1 is obviously (F, F).

Proposition 3.3 *In the counterfeiting game, a sub-game perfect Nash equilibrium is achieved at (F, F).*

Proof[16] We prove that F is a strictly dominant strategy for both firms.

---

[16] See Appendix 3.2 regarding a proof by calculations of profits.

52 K. DOMON

i. $\pi_{OO}^M < \pi_{FO}^M$

Under Firm L's Strategy O, Firm M selects either entering a middle-quality market (Strategy O) or both middle- and high-quality markets (Strategy F). Because Firm M can expand markets, she or he selects Strategy F to increase profits.

ii. $\pi_{OF}^M < \pi_{FF}^M$

Under Firm L's strategy F, Firm M selects either entering a middle-quality market (Strategy O) or both middle- and high-quality markets (Strategy F). Because Firm M loses profits from the high-quality market by Strategy O, she or he selects Strategy F to avoid profit decreases.

iii. $\pi_{OO}^L < \pi_{OF}^L$

Under Firm M's strategy O, Firm L selects either entering no other market (Strategy O) or both middle- and high-quality markets (Strategy F). Because Firm L can expand markets, she or he selects Strategy F to increase profits.

iv. $\pi_{FO}^L < \pi_{FF}^L$

Under Firm M's strategy F, Firm L selects entering either a low-quality market (Strategy O) or low-, middle-, and high-quality markets (Strategy F). Because Firm L loses profits from middle- and high-quality markets by Strategy O, she or he selects Strategy F to avoid profit decreases. □

We further consider incentives regarding perfect enforcement for counterfeiters. First, Firm L obviously does not see an incentive to perfect enforcement, since she or he always loses profits without entering into high- and middle-quality markets. On the other hand, Firm M experiences positive and negative effects of perfect enforcement on profits. She or he obtains benefits in a middle-quality market without counterfeits supplied by Firm L, while losing profits due to being excluded from the high-quality market. Which effect is greater depends on the situation of each market, expressed by the parameters.

Incentives for Counterfeiting

The profit of Firm M under perfect enforcement is

$$\pi_{OO}^M = \frac{(a^M - c^M)^2}{4b^M}, \tag{3.25}$$

which occurs in a middle-quality market without counterfeits supplied by Firm L. The profit under no enforcement is

$$\pi_{FF}^M = \frac{(a^H - 5c^M + c^L + 3c^H)^2}{36b_M^H} + \frac{(a^M - 2c^M + c^L)^2}{9b^M}, \qquad (3.26)$$

which consists of two terms. The first term is profit from counterfeit sales in the high-quality market, and the second is profit from non-counterfeit sales in the middle-quality market.

Proposition 3.4 *If and only if $\pi_{OO}^M > \pi_{FF}^M$, Firm M prefers perfect enforcement to no enforcement, although she or he cannot obtain it at a subgame perfect Nash equilibrium. Firm H always prefers perfect enforcement to no enforcement, and Firm L always prefers no enforcement to perfect enforcement.*

Proof This is obvious from the above discussions. □

This proposition indicates that a counterfeiter does not always desire lax enforcement. In reality, there are many levels of quality in counterfeits, and a simple competition between genuine and fake products is too simple to describe competition among various counterfeiters in terms of quality. We should notice the possibility that supply of relatively high-quality products using original brand names is hampered by lax enforcement. Since most high-quality products are supplied by foreign companies in developing countries, local authorities tend to avoid strict enforcement to benefit poor consumers and local industries. However, this proposition suggests that such a purpose prevents local producers from making profits by creating original brand names and fostering investment in R&D.

A numerical example helps us understand the concrete meaning of Proposition 3.3. Supposing $b^M = b_M^H = 1$, $c^H = 3$, $c^M = 2$, and $c^L = 1$, we obtain the following result,

$$(\pi_{OO}^M - \pi_{FF}^M) = \frac{(5a^M - 12)a^M - (a^H)^2}{36} \begin{Bmatrix} > \\ = \\ < \end{Bmatrix} 0$$

$$\Leftrightarrow a^H \begin{Bmatrix} > \\ = \\ < \end{Bmatrix} \sqrt{(5a^M - 12)a^M}. \qquad (3.27)$$

A relatively low value of a^H indicates that, under perfect enforcement, Firm M increases profits without counterfeits ($\pi_{OO}^M > \pi_{FF}^M$). In order for Firm M to prefer perfect enforcement, a^H must be relatively smaller than a^M. However, in this case, Firm M produces counterfeits under no enforcement as a result of the counterfeiting game.

Finally, this model can be extended to become a model with more than four firms producing products of different levels of quality. Here I have considered a model with the minimum number of firms playing a counterfeiting game. In the extension, we can consider various settings in which each counterfeiter decides which markets to enter.

Market Maturity Under Economic Growth

In order to check how the market has changed since 2011, we performed interviews again, in January 2016, with repairpersons and sellers in wholesale markets of spare parts.[17] We found a significant difference from our previous experience.

During this research, we saw original brand names of Thai companies and Vietnamese joint ventures with Taiwanese companies using original packages. This means that spare parts with original packages produced by such companies have gradually penetrated into the market.[18] According to repairpersons, customers have recently noticed that the quality of such spare parts is not bad, and they are acceptable to use. In previous research, we did not see repairpersons using second-tier original spare parts. They said last time that customers trusted only famous brand names and never bought spare parts packaged under unfamiliar brand names.

---

[17]We conducted interviews in eleven repair shops in Hanoi and Hai Phong and performed research at a black market, Cho Troi; a second-hand market, Chua Ha; and a wholesale market, Pho Hue, in Hanoi.

[18]We assume in our model that there is one producer in each market. However, in reality, there are many producers in each market. Some produce counterfeits and others originals of the same quality. In the wholesale market where we did research in 2016, seeking a spark plug and a chain, we could buy three levels of spare parts using the same packaging. Sellers told us that the lowest priced parts were fakes, and their quality was very low. This means that there are still counterfeiters, although we also see authentic spare parts in the second-tier spare parts market. That is, counterfeiters and original producers coexist in the market. Our model must be expanded if we need to consider such a situation in detail.

This change of consumers' evaluation of unknown brand names seems to be explained by experience goods over the long term. Consumers cannot quickly distinguish levels of quality and follow advice from repairpersons. Most consumers did not trust such advice when the package was unknown to them. Even in such situations, some tried to use unknown spare parts and noticed that they were of acceptable quality. Repairpersons said that they recommended unfamiliar brand spare parts when customers did not complain about the quality. Over the long term, customers have realized actual quality, and the second-tier spare part with an original package has penetrated into the market. Therefore, we have seen a process of expansion of real information among consumers over five years.

A second factor explaining the changing consumer evaluation is an increase in income. The annual economic growth rate in Vietnam from 2011 to 2015 was 6%.[19] Consumers can afford to purchase more expensive products than before. According to repairpersons, customers nowadays prefer a second-tier spare part to the cheapest one, though most still cannot afford to purchase first-tier parts. This means the second-tier market has expanded. Because of this expansion, spare parts made by Taiwanese and Thai companies have an opportunity to enter this market by using original brand names.

A final factor is enforcement. The level of enforcement has gone up, and counterfeit spare part makers in Vietnam are more frequently caught. We did not hear of such happenings in our 2011 and 2012 research. Under pressure from foreign governments for strict enforcement, Vietnamese authorities seem to have enforced protection of intellectual property rights by using the increased budget available due to economic growth, striving to catch counterfeiters. For example, a Taiwanese counterfeiter in Vietnam was caught by Vietnamese authorities.

In a real marketplace, these three factors seem to have contributed to growth of the market for second-tier spare parts with original brand names. In the economic model we have developed here, the influence of such factors is reflected in a relatively high a^M compared to a^H, where a producer of middle-quality spare parts needs strict enforcement to increase profits.

[19] See World Bank Statistics, http://data.worldbank.org/indicator/NY.GDP.MKTP.KD.ZG.

3.5 Concluding Remarks

Industrial goods like spare parts do not display the characteristics of bandwagon, snob, and Veblen effects on demand[20] that are seen in non-deceptive piracy. Counterfeits of spare parts are deceptive in general, but the meaning of the deception is not simple. I have explained that there are two kinds of deception, malicious and conscientious. Both are motivated by merits for repair shops in different situations.

Our first consideration here concerned conscientious deception. Under the assumption that consumers devalue national brands and do not trust a spare part with a national brand name, repair shops fill the information gap by indicating real value. In other words, domestic producers using fake packaging can survive and are helped in the market by repair shops' information intermediation. If counterfeits were perfectly enforced against, consumers would purchase only expensive foreign-brand spare parts, at least in the short run. In the long run, consumers gradually would realize the actual quality of domestic spare parts. However, in reality, under almost no enforcement, market equilibrium is achieved by using fake packages with intermediating real information from repair shops. An interesting result in this consideration is that real information about domestic spare parts damages foreign producers and possibly consumers buying foreign spare parts, yet totally increases domestic social welfare.

In the second consideration, in which consumers are cheated, we show that producers of relatively high-quality counterfeits have an incentive to produce originals under strict enforcement. However, in competition with low-quality counterfeit spare parts producers, a Nash equilibrium results in production of counterfeits. This offers a strategy for rights-holders to use, to convince authorities in developing countries that strict enforcement is necessary for promising domestic producers, as well as for consumers.

Authorities are said to realize the necessity of strict enforcement as economic development progresses, because consumers' preference for original products increases as incomes increase. Another explanation is

---

[20]See the seminal paper of Leibenstein (1950). Grossman and Shapiro (1988b) considered counterfeits with such characteristics in terms of an international trade problem.

that producers realize a prisoners' dilemma[21] in competition under no enforcement as industries mature. So producers themselves need protection of their trademarks.

Our result indicates, furthermore, that authorities should not only await such requests from consumers and producers, but also should ascertain whether counterfeiters producing relatively high-quality products need strict enforcement or not. Rights-holders can help authorities and convince them to implement strict enforcement. This situation creates an incentive that is compatible between developed and developing countries and that promotes the economic welfare of both countries. Finally, we should mention that market structures similar to that considered in our paper exist in other counterfeit markets.

APPENDIX

Appendix 3.1. Proof of $d\pi^{F*}/d\lambda < 0$.

$$\pi^{F*} = \left(p^{F*} - t^F\right)q^{F*} = \left(\frac{\bar{v}-1}{2}t^F - \frac{\lambda\bar{v}-1}{2}t^D\right)\left(\frac{\bar{v}}{2} - \frac{t^F - t^D}{2\Delta t}\right),$$

and we define

$$f(\lambda) \equiv \left(\frac{\bar{v}-1}{2}t^F - \frac{\lambda\bar{v}-1}{2}t^D\right) \quad \text{and} \quad g(\lambda) \equiv \left(\frac{\bar{v}}{2} - \frac{t^F - t^D}{2\Delta t}\right).$$

For a meaningful model, $f(\lambda) > 0$ and $g(\lambda) > 0$, and

$$\frac{df}{d\lambda} = -\frac{\bar{v}t^D}{2} < 0, \frac{dg}{d\lambda} = -\frac{\lambda\left(t^F - t^D\right)}{2\Delta t^2} < 0.$$

By using these results, we obtain

$$\frac{d\pi^{F*}}{d\lambda} = \frac{df}{d\lambda}g + f\frac{dg}{d\lambda} < 0. \qquad \square$$

---

[21] Note that our game is not a prisoners' dilemma game in which cooperation, i.e. strict enforcement, is beneficial for each producer.

58   K. DOMON

Appendix 3.2. Calculations of profits in Proposition 3.2.

The following conditions are satisfied by assumptions underlying the parameters:

$$\pi_{OO}^{M} < \pi_{FO}^{M} \iff 3c^{M} < a^{H} + 2c^{H},$$
$$\pi_{OF}^{M} < \pi_{FF}^{M} \iff 4c^{M} < a^{H} + 3c^{H},$$
$$\pi_{OO}^{L} < \pi_{OF}^{L} \iff 2c^{L} < a^{M} + c^{M}.$$

Regarding $\pi_{FO}^{L} < \pi_{FF}^{L}$, we must consider two markets, M and H markets, separately. If $2c^{L} < a^{M} + c^{M}$ for M market and $5c^{L} < a^{H} + 4c^{H}$ for H market, then $\pi_{FO}^{L} < \pi_{FF}^{L}$. From the parameters' assumptions, two inequalities in both markets are satisfied. □

REFERENCES

Chow, D. (2010). Anti-Counterfeiting Strategies of Multi-National Companies in China: How a Flawed Approach is Making Counterfeiting Worse. *Georgetown Journal of International Law, 41*, 749–779.

Darby, R. M., & Karni, E. (1973). Free Competition and the Optimal Amount of Fraud. *Journal of Law and Economics, 16*(1), 67–88.

Dulleck, U., & Kerschbamer, R. (2006). On Doctors, Mechanics, and Computer Specialists: The Economics of Credence Goods. *Journal of Economic Literature, 44*(1), 5–42.

Fujita, M. (2007). *Local Firms in Latecomer Developing Countries Amidst China's Rise: The Case of Vietnam's Motorcycle Industry* (Discussion Paper 97). Institute of Developing Economies.

Fujita, M. (2008). *Value Chain Dynamics and Growth of Local Firms: The Case of Motorcycle Industry in Vietnam* (Discussion Paper 161). Institute of Developing Economies.

Grossman, G. M., & Shapiro, C. (1988a). Counterfeit-Product Trade. *American Economic Review, 78*, 59–75.

Grossman, G. M., & Shapiro, C. (1988b). Foreign Counterfeiting of Status Goods. *Quarterly Journal of Economics, 103*, 79–100.

Higgins, S. R., & Rubin, P. H. (1986). Counterfeit Goods. *Journal of Law and Economics, 29*(2), 211–230.

Hung, C. L. (2003). The Business of Product Counterfeiting in China and the Post-WTO Membership Environment. *Asia Pacific Business Review, 10*(1), 58–77.

Kaikati, J. G., & LaGarce, R. (1980). Beware of International Brand Piracy. *Harvard Business Review, 58*(2), 52.

Leibenstein, H. (1950). Bandwagon, Snob, and Veblen Effects in the Theory of Consumers' Demand. *Quarterly Journal of Economics, 64*(2), 183–207.

Minagawa, T., Trott, P., & Hoecht, A. (2007). Counterfeit, Imitation, Reverse Engineering and Learning: Reflections from Chinese Manufacturing Firms. *R&D Management, 37*(5), 455–467.

Olsen, J. E., & Granzin, K. L. (1993). Using Channel Constructs to Explain Dealers' Willingness to Help Manufacturers Combat Counterfeiting. *Journal of Business Research, 27*, 147–170.

Ramello, G. B. (2006). What's in a Sign? Trademark Law and Economic Theory. *Journal of Economic Surveys, 20*(4), 547–565.

Staake, T., Thiesse, F., & Fleisch, E. (2009). The Emergence of Counterfeit Trade: A Literature Review. *European Journal of Marketing, 43*(3), 320–349.

CHAPTER 4

Markets of Quasi-Credence and Similar Foods

Abstract This chapter considers quasi-credence and similar foods in Southeast Asian countries. In a market of foreign foods (quasi-credence foods) where domestic consumers cannot distinguish counterfeits from originals even after eating them, domestic authorities do not have an incentive for enforcement if originals are not produced in the country, that is, if profits of an original producer do not contribute to domestic social welfare. An incentive for strict enforcement exists only if originals are produced in the country. I also consider a market of similar processed foods, where judgement about design right infringement is vague. Some companies sue, and others do not respond to the infringement. I consider this phenomenon by using a model of monopolistic competition and prove that the similarity can create positive mutual externalities and benefit all producers. This outcome parallels a form of biological mimicry (Müllerian mimicry).

Keywords Batesian mimicry · Experience food · Quasi-credence food · Müllerian mimicry

4.1 Background

This chapter addresses trade in counterfeited and non-original Japanese food and ingredients in a sample of three Southeast Asian countries: Vietnam, Thailand, and Indonesia. By means of questionnaires and

© The Author(s) 2018
K. Domon, *An Economic Analysis of Intellectual Property Rights Infringement*, Palgrave Studies in Institutions, Economics and Law,
https://doi.org/10.1007/978-3-319-90466-5_4

61

interviews with staff working at Japanese restaurants, the study tries to understand the reasons why non-original ingredients are, in certain circumstances, used despite the expectations of customers, and to identify the main economic reasons explaining this apparently widespread phenomenon. Accordingly, Japanese authorities are considering how to solve this problem in order to promote exports of original Japanese food and ingredients. Under these circumstances, from November 2013 to March 2015, I visited local Japanese restaurants, marketplaces, customs offices at borders, and authorities in Southeast Asia.[1]

I focus on counterfeits of Japanese food and ingredients used in Japanese restaurants. There are two kinds of Japanese food and ingredients in terms of the place of production. Most are produced in Japan, but there are also local producers run by Japanese companies. For example, a typical Japanese ingredient, a soy sauce, is produced in several countries in Southeast Asia.

In general, counterfeit products are classified into two categories, deceptive and non-deceptive. While both kinds of counterfeit products damage original producers, non-deceptive counterfeits do not harm consumers. Counterfeit foods belong to the class of deceptive goods,[2] since consumers are not willing to purchase foods with health risks. Regarding deception involving product quality, Darby and Karni (1973) raised the matter of "credence quality", which is expensive to judge, even after purchase, affecting perceptions of whether a product is authentic or not. As we will explain below, counterfeits of Japanese food apparently have such characteristics for local people.

Regarding credence goods in food markets, there are many discussions of labelling to reduce incomplete information about quality. Using spatial price discrimination models where consumers distribute along a line with a uniform distribution, Giannakas (2002) created a simulation

---

[1] This field research at retailers, wholesalers, and suppliers in Vietnam, Thailand, Malaysia, and Singapore was done in December 2013, and research regarding border trade among Thailand, Myanmar, and Laos; between Singapore and Indonesia; and between Vietnam and China, in February 2014. Survey data were collected in Indonesia in July 2014 and in Thailand and Vietnam in August and September 2014. Questionnaires were collected door-to-door by local research assistants directly from Japanese restaurants.

[2] Higgins and Rubin (1986) considered the snob effect of brand name products on counterfeiting. However, with food products this effect is minor, and we need not take it into account.

to analyse the effects of mislabelling on economic welfare, indicating insufficient regulation of labelling. Fulton and Giannakas (2004) developed a market model that considered both consumers' and producers' behaviours in detail, describing complicated incentives influencing them. Bonroy and Constantos (2008) further developed a model of Gabszewicz and Grilo (1992) and showed that a high-quality producer may not have an incentive to introduce regulation of labels and that mandatory regulation may be necessary.

In a non-spatial model of price discrimination, Anania and Nisticò (2004) considered the effects of public enforcement upon cheating behaviours, which depend on the level of suppliers' risk aversion, and indicated an incentive for producers to support a degree of regulation of labels. Vetter and Karantininis (2002) also considered how vertical integration or divestiture of a processed food firm is effective in coping with credence quality. In such articles, costs of enforcement and monitoring by authorities are assumed to be covered by fines, or food processors can obtain the public information freely. That is, the level of enforcement and monitoring can be exogenously determined and adjusted. However, for authorities in developing countries, confronting many social problems to be solved, costs are critical and budgets limited, and they do not have the free hand such models assume.[3]

The deceptive counterfeits considered here are more harmful to both consumers and original producers than the credence products discussed in the above articles, since counterfeiters intentionally break intellectual property laws. Through a distribution system, producers of low-quality and unsafe foods and ingredients copy an original and sell it as an original. After producing such foods, trade is conducted in complicated hidden distribution channels, mostly beyond borders, in Southeast Asia.[4] In interviews investigating trade in counterfeit foods, I met with

---

[3] For example, in Vietnam, effective enforcement by authorities is financially supported by foreign companies producing original products. Without such support, authorities cannot enforce trade rules, due to manpower and budget constraints. We heard about concrete measures undertaken with local authorities to combat counterfeits from several Japanese companies.

[4] A typical case we saw in interviews is that a package copied from an original is produced in China and smuggled into neighbouring countries, where counterfeit foods using brand names are sold. There are fake soy sauces, cooking sake, MSG (monosodium glutamate), and so on, using such packages. The risk of being detected at borders and the transport cost of smuggling finished counterfeit foods from China negatively impact profits. Consequently, counterfeiting industries are often internationally divided due to strict border enforcement.

participants engaged in the supply chain. Actual trade in counterfeit foods is not as simple as the typical market, consisting of merely producers and consumers, that economic theory describes. The study of real marketplaces where incomplete information in trade takes place is a complicated task, depending upon which kinds of foods are considered and where in the supply chain a particular trade is taking place. Through interviews with wholesalers, importers, retailers, and restaurants, I looked into the workings of such marketplaces.

The main agent dealing with Japanese foods and ingredients is an importer. There are several methods of importation. Most retailers and restaurants purchase from major importers or so-called suppliers. There are a few major suppliers in Vietnam, Thailand, and Indonesia, periodically importing by cargo ship. They do not usually deal with counterfeit foods and are trusted by all consumers and restaurants. In most cases, the price of such imported foods is much higher than the original price in Japan. Therefore, the price is very high compared to the local price level.

In addition, there are many small and medium-sized suppliers dealing with counterfeit foods and ingredients. Their targets are those inexpensive restaurants to which ordinary local people can afford to go. Since imported Japanese foods are very expensive, such restaurants are always trying to obtain these foods as cheaply as they can. I heard, in interviews with suppliers and restaurants, that such suppliers deal with counterfeit foods deceptively, and some restaurants are being cheated, buying counterfeits as low-priced originals.

Behind this deception, there are two stages in the supply chain where incomplete information occurs. One is between suppliers and restaurants, and the other is between restaurants and customers. Most suppliers have correct information on whether food is counterfeit or not, but cheap restaurants with local staff and owners find authenticity difficult to judge. Even if Japanese employees in such restaurants can judge flavour accurately, the local owners are willing to buy cheap foods and ingredients that may include counterfeits. This asymmetric information stems from the experience of cooking and eating authentic Japanese food.[5] Without training for a long time, local chefs and owners cannot

---

[5] I heard in interviews conducted in several restaurants that, even though Japanese chefs teach local staff the taste of Japanese cuisine, they soon forget it and must be checked regularly, for example, every month. This suggests that non-Japanese chefs are not accustomed to authentic Japanese tastes and find them difficult to realize. This is a natural phenomenon around the world and also valid with respect to other countries' tastes, i.e. it is a credence quality.

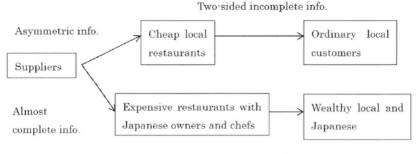

Fig. 4.1 Structure of incomplete information

distinguish original foods from counterfeits. On the other side, most suppliers have information on a product's source even though they do not have knowledge of an authentic Japanese taste. That is, asymmetric information exists between suppliers and restaurants (Fig. 4.1).

The second stage of incomplete information, between restaurants and customers, is symmetric. Since many low-income local customers who go to cheap Japanese restaurants have not often tasted authentic Japanese foods, they do not know if restaurants use original Japanese ingredients and foods or not. On the other hand, inexpensive restaurants may be cheated by suppliers. Therefore, both sides face incomplete information. Such a situation does not seriously damage either restaurants or customers, as long as the counterfeit foods are safe and their prices are reasonable. Moreover, customers can afford to enjoy Japanese (or "Japanese") flavours, and restaurants can make profits. However, original producers are damaged. This two-sided incomplete information has the same property as that of non-deceptive counterfeits in terms of damage to original producers.

In interviews,[6] we heard that local people have difficulty judging authentic Japanese foods and ingredients. Several major suppliers dealing only with originals know the details of competitors, especially small suppliers who sell counterfeits, invading original food markets. They say that small suppliers, who can be contacted only by mobile phone, target small and cheap restaurants, selling counterfeits as authentic foods with low prices by door-to-door sales (asymmetric information).[7] We saw

---

[6] I did interviews at 26 places in Indonesia, 17 in Vietnam, and 10 in Thailand.

[7] While small suppliers do not have a space or a store to show the goods they deal in, major suppliers run grocery stores where buyers can check quality.

many small Japanese restaurants owned by local people who could not detect counterfeits unless/until a Japanese customer questioned a product's quality (two-sided incomplete information).

4.2   QUASI-CREDENCE FOOD

Incentives of Authorities

Credence food is defined as a food product whose quality cannot be identified even after consumption. A typical example is generic modified food. There is another type of credence food. Local consumers who are not accustomed to an original quality lack the knowledge to judge originals. For them, before experiencing an original version of a food, that food is a credence product. A typical example is a seasoning like a soy sauce or an olive oil. Only after becoming accustomed to original foods can a consumer judge originals. I shall call such a food a quasi-credence food.

In Asia, there are many low-priced Japanese restaurants whose chefs and customers do not have the knowledge to distinguish originals from counterfeits. Quasi-credence foods are widespread, and there are counterfeits with well-known brand names among them. Unlike in spare parts markets, producers and retailers of such foods do not have any incentive to provide accurate quality information to buyers and consumers, who are perfectly cheated. Those who want to use cheap foodstuffs and enjoy inexpensive dishes with affordable prices are likely to evaluate quasi-credence counterfeits higher than the real product.

In order to analyse a market of quasi-credence foods, a spatial model such as was used in Section 3.3 is useful. A difference from the previous model is the parameter λ, which was less than 1. Counterfeits as quasi-credence foods are generally overestimated by buyers and consumers, while domestic spare parts are generally underestimated by consumers.

Here, I introduce $\gamma(\geq 1)$ instead of $\lambda(\leq 1)$ and substitute a superscript F for O (Original) and D for C (Counterfeit). γ indicates the difference in an evaluation of counterfeit food between time before and time after knowing authentic taste, and does not mean the level of law enforcement. Consumers can select either high-price (originals) or low-price food. Under no enforcement, low-price food is sold as original with well-known brand names (counterfeiting) and $\gamma > 1$.[8] Under perfect enforcement, it is sold as original low-quality food, $\gamma = 1$, and consumers do not overestimate it. Overestimation of quality in quasi-credence food is caused only by a well-known foreign brand name. Without it, consumers do not overestimate domestic food. Unlike domestic spare parts (experience goods with a bad image), perfect law enforcement can be effective to make $\gamma = 1$ in the short run. I will consider perfect imitation in Section 4.3. Here, I consider results from the characteristics of quasi-credence goods to be different from those of experience goods.

Although consumers are perfectly cheated before having authentic food, an overestimation of counterfeit food makes consumers' surplus high, original producer's profits small, and domestic economic welfare high.[9] If the originals are produced abroad, domestic social welfare is defined as $SW^D \equiv CS^O + CS^C$, increasing with γ. If the originals are domestic products, social welfare is defined as $SW \equiv PS^O + CS^O + CS^C$ due to $PS^C = 0$, decreasing with γ.[10] That is,

Proposition 4.1 *In a quasi-credence food market, $\frac{dSW}{d\gamma} < 0$, if $\frac{1}{2} t^c (\tilde{v}^2 - \underline{v}^2) < -(p^{O*} - t^O)\frac{dq^{O*}}{d\gamma}$, and $\frac{dSW^D}{d\gamma} > 0$ for all γ. That is, for domestic authorities, the nationality of an original producer is a criterion for strict enforcement. Only if originals are produced by domestic producers, is there a possibility that they have an incentive for perfect enforcement ($\gamma = 1$).*

Proof See Appendix 4.1.

In the case of a domestic original producer, this suggests that a decrease in the original producer's profit along with γ could not be compensated by an increase in consumers' surplus along with γ. As a result, perfect enforcement, $\gamma = 1$, might be best for authorities. This suggests that an incentive for perfect enforcement for quasi-credence goods might grow stronger along with the development of domestic producers creating their own brand names.

---

[8] In cheap local Japanese restaurants, I could see bottles of soy sauce on the tables with original brand names, but the taste was strange to me. Local customers, like the guides accompanying me, could not notice a taste difference. The staff of the restaurant probably bought soy sauce at a low price from a small supplier, although the staff could have bought at a high price from a reliable supplier.

[9] These results can be obtained as in Section 3.3.

[10] We must take into account an effect of γ on p^{O*} and, therefore, on $U_i^O = t^O v_i - p^{O*}$, and cannot graphically obtain these outcomes only from Fig. 4.2.

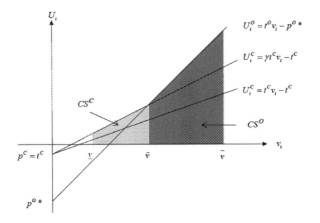

Fig. 4.2 Market equilibrium under quasi-credence food

In the actual marketplace, suppliers and traders are intermediate between consumers and producers. I interviewed staff of major suppliers trading only in original foreign food. They complained about counterfeits of famous foreign food that competed with originals and damaged their businesses. When we take into account such domestic suppliers, the incentives of authorities for perfect enforcement are reinforced.

Comparing this result with discussions about a bad image of domestic products in the previous chapter, we notice an interesting fact. In spare parts markets, domestic authorities have an incentive for perfect enforcement to maximize domestic social welfare, $CS^D + CS^F$. Here, in quasi-credence food markets, they do not have an incentive for enforcement to increase $CS^O + CS^C$. In a real marketplace of spare parts, as explained in the previous chapter, not authorities but repair shops mitigate incomplete information on quality, and their behaviours work well, although they do not perfectly fill information gaps. In real food marketplaces including restaurants, I could not see such behaviours at all. Most consumers are perfectly cheated. Ironically, such a situation is best[11] as long as original producers do not include a domestic company.[12]

---

[11] If we consider a risky food for health, this result is not valid. A typical case is a counterfeit of expensive foreign whisky. Authorities in ASEAN have strictly enforced such counterfeits due to many fatal incidents.

[12] Some foreign ingredients and processed foods are produced by domestic companies. Such foods are considered as quasi-credence goods.

Domestic Food as Experience Goods

In the above discussion, I defined foreign food as quasi-credence goods. We can often see counterfeit food with domestically well-known brand names,[13] a type of experience goods for domestic consumers, since they can distinguish counterfeits from originals after eating. I briefly consider such food for comparison with quasi-credence food.

Figure 4.3 shows an equilibrium and consumers' surpluses in an experience foods market. Due to experience with the food, consumers who buy counterfeit s notice the real quality after eating, and some, locating in $\left[\tilde{v}|_{\gamma=1}, \tilde{v}\right]$, regret the purchase of cheap food, while others, locating in $[\underline{v}, \tilde{v}|_{\gamma=1}]$, still prefer cheap food, but are damaged. Such consumers are considered victims of a market distortion resulting from incomplete information about quality. We can obtain the following clear result,

Proposition 4.2 *In an experience food market,* SW *is maximized for* $\gamma = 1$.

Proof See Appendix 4.2.

If there is no foreign producer, then policymakers must always consider domestic producers and consumers. In such cases, complete information with no market distortion is obviously best.

4.3   A NEGATIVE FREQUENCY-DEPENDENT SELECTION IN IMITATED FOODS

In a given market, we see many similar packages of famous processed food, like snack food. In Southeast Asia, SMEs imitate and legally supply famous foreign snack foods. Visiting foreigners can see a variety of such foods with similar tastes and packages. Most were first supplied before foreign original producers entered the market in developing countries. For example, a famous Japanese snack, first produced in the 1960s, was imitated by a Thai local company. The original has a unique shape that is difficult to produce, but the company imported a food processing

---

[13] Data in Baroncelli et al. (2005) indicate how many trademarks owned by foreign companies in developed countries are registered in developing countries. Concerning the trend in Chinese and Indian trademarks, see Godinho and Ferreira (2012).

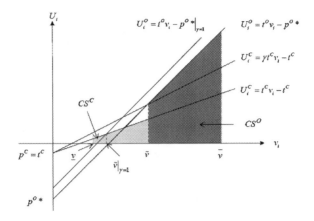

Fig. 4.3 Market equilibrium for experience foods

machine that was invented by a Japanese machine-builder. In those days, snack food companies did not make much use of patents in order to protect their food processing machines, and the Thai company could imitate the shape and package of the famous snack food, but could not produce the same taste as the original. However, because of the unique shape and taste, it was a hit and is still popular. Now, there are several similar snack foods, creating a category of snack foods. One problem of such similar processing of foods is illegality. Original producers do not always accept such foods and sometimes sue imitating companies. Whether a suit takes place or not depends first on the infringement of a design right and/or a trademark, and second on the influence on the original producer's profits.

Phenomena occurring in a market of similar snack foods resemble mimicry among insects. In biological evolution, mimicry is a common phenomenon to escape predators. A model that receives less attack from predators due to an appearance signalling danger or a bad taste is imitated in its appearance by a mimic. Mimicry takes Batesian and Müllerian forms.[14]

In Batesian mimicry, mimics with a taste favoured by a predator imitate a model carrying an unpalatable taste or a toxic substance, cheating

---

[14] See Chapters 10 and 11 of Ruxton et al. (2004) and Ohzaki (2009).

the predator. In this case, only mimics have benefits from imitation, while increasing the rate of models attacked by predators. This phenomenon that the attack rate of models increases along with the number of mimics, balancing when the attack rate of models is equal to that of mimics, is called a *negative frequency-dependent selection.*

Regarding similar snack foods, an original producer and an imitator correspond, respectively, to a model and a mimic, and a consumer is a predator. A difference between biological mimicry[15] and food similarity is that an original producer (a model) benefits from consumption (an attack). In such an economic interpretation, consumers' demand decreases along with the amount of similar foods or the number of producers. In equilibrium, an original producer must survive in the market because a fake producer cannot sell products without originals. That is, in a market with all low-quality imitations, market demand is insufficient to make profits.

In order to analyse the equilibrium, I set up the following model. An inverse demand function is,

$$p = \frac{a}{n} - \frac{b}{n} \sum_{i=1}^{n} q_i, \tag{4.1}$$

where p is a market price and q_i $(i=1, 2, ..., n)$ the amount of firm i's products. Here, there are an original producer and $(n-1)$ fake producers. a and b are strictly positive parameters. When we interpret the inverse demand function as a marginal utility function, it expresses an expected marginal utility if the value of a fake is zero. In a symmetric situation, the market share of original products[16] is $1/n$.

An original producer's profit is

$$\pi_1 = \left(\frac{a}{n} - \frac{b}{n} \sum_{i=1}^{n} q_i \right) q_1 - f - cq_1 \tag{4.2}$$

---

[15] See Watt (2011) regarding an analogy of biological prey–predator behaviours to an economic model of copyright.

[16] Assuming a quasi-linear utility function, $U = v(Q) - pQ$ where $Q = \sum_{i=1}^{n} q_i$ and $v(Q) = \left\{ a \cdot Q - \frac{b}{2} \cdot Q^2 \right\} / n$. I obtain the first-order condition of utility maximization with respect to Q, $p = \frac{a}{n} - b \cdot Q/n$.

72   K. DOMON

An original producer is indexed as Firm 1, and others as Firms 2, ..., n. f and c are respectively a fixed cost and a marginal cost. Only an original producer has the fixed cost of producing and maintaining a high-quality product. A fake producer's profit is

$$\pi_i = \left(\frac{a}{n} - \frac{b}{n} \sum_{j=1}^{n} q_j \right) q_i - c q_i, \text{ for } i = 2, 3, \ldots, n. \tag{4.3}$$

Except for fixed costs, an original and a fake producer face the same situation. In order to solve this game concretely, symmetry is necessary.

A Nash equilibrium is obtained as follows,

$$q^N = \frac{a - cn}{b(n+1)}, \tag{4.4}$$

where $q^N = q_i^N$ ($i=1, 2, \ldots, n$). Denoting market supply and price as, respectively, Q^N and p^N at this equilibrium, we obtain that both an original and a fake producer's profit, as well as consumers' surpluses, defined as

$$CS^N \equiv \int_0^{Q^N} p \, dQ - p^N Q^N, \tag{4.5}$$

and producers' surpluses, defined as

$$PS^N \equiv \sum_{i=1}^{n} \pi_i^N, \tag{4.6}$$

decrease with n.

Proposition 4.3 $\pi_i^N (i = 1, 2, \ldots, n)$, CS^N and PS^N are strictly decreasing with n.

Proof $\pi_1^N = \frac{A}{bn} - f$, $\pi_i^N = \frac{A}{bn}$, ($i=2, 3, \ldots, n$), $CS^N = \frac{A}{2b}$, and $PS^N = \frac{A}{b} - f$, where $A = \left(\frac{a-c}{n+1} \right)^2$. Since $dA/dn < 0$, $d\pi_i^N/dn < 0$ ($i = 1, 2, \ldots, n$), $dCS^N/dn < 0$, and $dPS^N/dn < 0$. $\qquad\square$

In a usual oligopoly without a fake product, entry of newcomers into a market increases social welfare, $SW = CS + PS$, as well as CS, by a certain level. However, in this model, demand shrinkage resulting from a fake product causes a decrease in CS, resulting in a decrease in SW. The discount effect caused by a new entry cannot compensate for the shrink in demand. It is easy to ascertain that this result is valid if a fake product has less value than an original one. This explains the necessary illegality of imitation products.

Under no law enforcement, fake producers enter the market as long as they can make positive profits. However, without an original producer, consumers do not buy any products, and the market disappears. A threshold for an original's zero profit is obtained as follows.

Proposition 4.4 (Threshold of Market Existence) *There exists an $n(\equiv n^*)$ satisfying $q^N = \sqrt{nf/b}$ where $\pi_1^N = 0$ and $\pi_{i\neq 1}^N > 0$, and n^* is strictly decreasing with f.*

Proof $\pi_1^N = \frac{b}{n}(q^N)^2 - f$, and, when $\pi_1^N = 0$, $q^N = \sqrt{nf/b}$ must be satisfied. Since q^N is strictly decreasing with x and $\sqrt{nf/b}$ is strictly increasing with x, there is a n^*. Because q^N is independent of f and $\sqrt{nf/b}$ is strictly increasing with f, n^* is strictly decreasing with f. $\qquad\square$

This proposition indicates that, under free entry and no enforcement, fake producers make strictly positive profits while an original producer's profit is zero at equilibrium. This result is different from a usual oligopoly under free entry where all symmetric producers' profits are zero. The market share of an original product goes down from 1 to $1/n^*$ in the long run (a negative frequency-dependent selection).

4.4 A POSITIVE FREQUENCY-DEPENDENT SELECTION IN SIMILAR FOODS

In Müllerian mimicry, the shape and colour of an unpalatable model are imitated by other insects, and the group of insects effectively escapes attack by predators. Since predators learn of a bad taste after eating some insects, the probability within the group of being eaten is reduced. Group members utilize a positive mutual externality. A similar positive externality is also created in snack food industries. The probability of consumption may increase when consumers have more chances to see a similar kind of snack foods, and a consumer who has learned of a good taste is also likely to try other similar products. This is considered a promotion effect by similarity.[17]

I assume that an imitated product differs from a similar one. In the case of an imitation, counterfeiters cheat consumers by selling a low-quality product as an original in order to make profits. There is always such an incentive for counterfeiters who find no merit in producing products of the same quality as the original. However, regarding a similar product, most consumers realize differences from the original.[18] When difference is unrecognizable, a similar product should be treated as an imitation even if the product has a real difference from the original. A similar package is often problematic and can be sued for a design right infringement, but whether a similar product infringes a design right or not can be difficult to judge.

A similar product is considered to demonstrate product differentiation while an imitation is considered a homogeneous product except for quality. To analyse the similar product market in the food industry, I use Dixit-Stiglitz's CES utility function. A representative consumer has the following utility function,

$$
U = \left(\sum_{i=1}^{n} q_i^{\rho} \right)^{\frac{1}{\rho}},
\tag{4.7}
$$

where $0 < \rho < 1$, and a budget constraint,

$$
I = \sum_{i=1}^{n} p_i q_i + s/n,
\tag{4.8}
$$

where s is the cost for consumers to encounter at least one among n differentiated goods, and I is a consumer's budget. The cost is interpreted as a kind of search cost to know of the group. With increasing n, an original and its similar products increase the chance of an encounter in the market, and the cost decreases. An abundance of differentiated goods as a whole plays the role of advertisement to consumers.

[17] As Landes and Posner explain (1987), an efficient transmission of information quality is one of the important roles of trademarks. A similar shape and package work like a joint trademark.

[18] Mealem et al. (2010) analysed trademark infringement and obtain unique results under an assumption that the quality of a counterfeit has the same quality as that of an original, that is, a perfect substitute with no damage to consumers. It is very strong assumption.

In a symmetric situation, each producer sets the same price, and a consumer buys the same amount of goods. Therefore, in any market equilibrium, $p_i = p$ and $q_i = q$ $(i = 1, 2, \ldots, n)$, and $I = npq + s/n$.

Proposition 4.5 *Given p, demand increases if and only if $s/I < n < 2s/I$.*

Proof From the budget constraint, $q = \frac{I}{pn} - \frac{s}{pn^2}$, and $\frac{\partial q}{\partial n} = \frac{1}{pn^2}\left(\frac{2s}{n} - I\right)$. Therefore, $\partial q / \partial n > 0 \Leftrightarrow n < 2s/I$. Moreover, $n > s/I$ because of $q > 0$. □

This proposition explains that a positive externality of a new entry towards demand takes place in a certain interval of n, which depends on the ratio of s to I. Since there is always a negative externality if $s = 0$, this positive externality compensates for the demerit of a new entry. In Fig. 4.4, the area in which demand increases is depicted by Area I. Since there must be a competition, $n \geq 2$. For example, $4 < n < 8$ if $I = s/4$.

I consider more details regarding the impact of n on profits. A consumer's demand is obtained by solving the following problem,

$$\underset{q_i}{\text{Max}} \left(\sum_{i=1}^{n} q_i^\rho\right)^{\frac{1}{\rho}} \quad \text{s.t.} \ I = \sum_{i=1}^{n} p_i q_i + s/n. \tag{4.9}$$

From the first-order condition for utility maximization, I obtain a usual condition as follows,

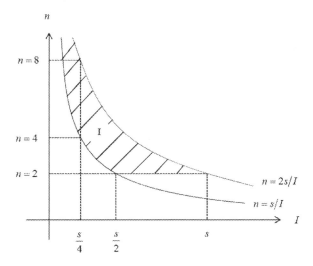

Fig. 4.4 Area of demand expansion

$$q_i = q_j \cdot \left(\frac{p_j}{p_i}\right)^{\frac{1}{1-\rho}}. \tag{4.10}$$

Inserting this into the budget constraint equation, I obtain a demand function as follows,

$$q_j = \left(I - \frac{s}{n}\right) \frac{p_j^{-\sigma}}{\sum_{i=1}^{n} p_i^{1-\sigma}}, \quad \left(\sigma = \frac{1}{1-\rho} > 1\right). \tag{4.11}$$

Under the assumption that strategic factors in $\sum_{i=1}^{n} p_i^{1-\sigma} (\equiv k)$ are negligible or constant for each producer (monopolistic competition), interactions in the game disappear and the problem of profit maximization is easily solved. A representative producer's profit is defined as follows,

$$\pi = pq - f - cq = (p - c)\left(I - \frac{s}{n}\right)\frac{p^{-\sigma}}{k} - f, \tag{4.12}$$

where f and c are, respectively, a fixed and a marginal cost. The profit is maximized at $p^* = c\sigma/(\sigma - 1)$, which does not depend on n.

Proposition 4.6 (Positive mutual externality) *In an equilibrium, profit increases with n if and only if $s/I < n < 2s/I$, and utility does so if and only if $n > s/I$.*

Proof In an equilibrium, profit and its derivative are

$$\pi^* = (p^* - c)\left(I - \frac{s}{n}\right)\frac{p^{*-\sigma}}{np^{*1-\sigma}} - f = \frac{p^* - c}{np^*}\left(I - \frac{s}{n}\right) - f,$$

$$\frac{\partial \pi^*}{\partial n} = \frac{p^* - c}{p^* n^2}\left(\frac{2s}{n} - I\right).$$

Therefore, $\partial \pi^*/\partial n > 0 \Leftrightarrow n < 2s/I$. Moreover, $n > s/I$ because consumer demand must be strictly positive; that is,

$$q^* = \frac{I}{p^* n} - \frac{s}{p^* n^2} > 0.$$

Utility is

$$U^* = \left(\sum_{i=1}^{n} q_i^{*\rho} \right)^{\frac{1}{\rho}} = \left\{ \left(I - \frac{s}{n} \right) \middle/ p^* \right\}^{\frac{1}{\rho}}.$$

$$\frac{\partial U^*}{\partial n} = \frac{1}{\rho} \left\{ \frac{1}{\rho} \left(I - \frac{s}{n} \right) \right\}^{\frac{1}{\rho} - 1} \frac{s}{p^{*\frac{1}{\rho}} n^2}.$$

Because p^* is independent of n and $1/\rho - 1 > 0$, $\partial U^*/\partial n > 0$ if and only if $n > s/I$ $(q > 0)$. $\qquad\square$

From Propositions 4.5 and 4.6, the interval for a demand expansion corresponds to that for a profit increase. $\partial \pi^*/\partial n < 0$ for any n if $s=0$, but a similarity brings about positive mutual externalities in the early stage of a market entry if $s > 0$. If n increases beyond $2s/I$, π^* decreases. Unlike the imitation, a consumer's utility, U^*, increases with n. At least for $s/I < n < 2s/I$, social welfare increases with n, and a similar product benefits not only the consumer, but also each producer.

4.5 Actual Trade of Counterfeit Japanese Food

Using interviews and questionnaires,[19] we can realize how incomplete information plays out in an actual foreign market for Japanese food. Herein, I present data related to this discussion.

The first data concern the relationship between imitation foods and Japanese staff. Because of the popularity of Japanese food, there are many restaurants whose owners and/or staff have no relationship to Japan and can only imitate tastes and atmosphere without authentic knowledge. This phenomenon occurs not only with Japanese food, but is also common with other foreign food. In the data below, more than 50% of restaurants do not have any Japanese staff. Because of the high wage commanded by Japanese staff, it is difficult for cheap restaurants to hire them. In interviews in such shops, I saw local owners and staff who had worked in Japanese restaurants and opened their own restaurants. Some had not experienced training and had only lived in Japan. Such restaurants could be run by imitating Japanese taste. The percentages of restaurants that had Japanese chefs were 35.1% in Indonesia, 27.3%

---

[19]We collected 46 samples in Indonesia (I), 115 in Thailand (T), and 62 in Vietnam (V). They were collected by directly visiting restaurants from July to September in 2014.

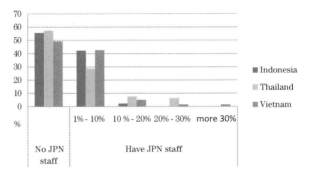

Fig. 4.5 Percentage of Japanese staff

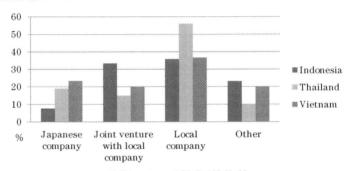

Fig. 4.6 Ownership of Japanese restaurants

in Thailand, and 23.0% in Vietnam. Ownership is shown in Fig. 4.6. Percentages of local companies are largest, reflecting the data in Fig. 4.5.

Next, let us examine procurement of ingredients. As explained in Section 4.1, there are small and medium-sized suppliers dealing with counterfeits, major suppliers dealing only with authentic ingredients, and Japanese companies importing directly from Japan. Trade of counterfeits mostly takes place among small and medium-sized suppliers. In Fig. 4.7, such suppliers are included among local import traders and local dealers. The data show that most restaurants depend on them. It is unlikely that this phenomenon takes place only in Japanese food restaurants and not also in other foreign restaurants. Counterfeits were found to be evenly

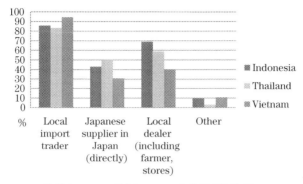

Multiple answers, Valid response: I=42, T=102, V=55

Fig. 4.7 Channels of ingredient procurement

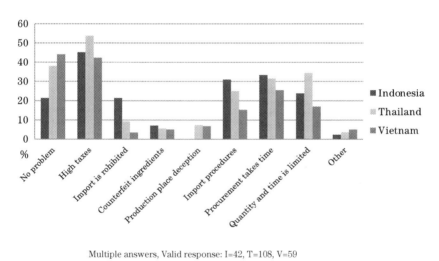

Multiple answers, Valid response: I=42, T=108, V=59

Fig. 4.8 Problems regarding Japanese ingredients

distributed in various places, and rates of finding counterfeits were about 20% in each country: 15.2% in Indonesia, 22.6% in Thailand, and 20.9% in Vietnam. Compared to the percentages in developed countries, where we hardly see counterfeit foods, those percentages are very high.

Figure 4.8 shows problems obtaining Japanese ingredients and foods. Counterfeit problems do not rank highly. The most serious problem is high tax. But the high tax causes a high price and creates a high return from making counterfeits. Those reporting a counterfeit problem were 7.1% in Indonesia, 5.6% in Thailand, and 5.1% in Vietnam.

4.6   Concluding Remarks

Those who have never eaten an authentic version of a foreign meal cannot distinguish a counterfeit food from an authentic one even after eating. To realize an authentic taste, customers need to eat authentic food several times. For example, in Southeast Asia, the rich who travel to Japan many times are sensitive to authenticity because they can judge real Japanese tastes. On the other hand, in food courts and cheap restaurants, ordinary people, who do not have any experience eating authentic Japanese food, enjoy localized versions as Japanese dishes. For these consumers, it is not authenticity but Japanese style and atmosphere that are important. For profitable counterfeiting, such customers are necessary.

The phenomenon of quasi-credence goods creates a controversial problem that customers overestimate the value of counterfeits and cannot be aware of actual value. In such a case, I have proven that the total of consumers' surpluses stemming from originals and counterfeits increases with overestimation. Domon et al. (2018) statistically show that Japanese restaurants attract customers by creating a Japanese atmosphere. Most of the customers cannot distinguish originals from counterfeits. In addition, if the producer of originals is a foreign company, domestic social welfare can be increased with overestimation. Therefore, domestic authorities do not have an incentive to enforce counterfeits. However, the story is different if domestic original producers' intellectual property rights are infringed by domestic counterfeiters and if perfect enforcement makes customers notice counterfeits. Such cases will be created when a developing country like Vietnam develops to a level at least close to that of an emerging country.

A similar processed food, which is not a counterfeit because consumers can identify one or more differences from the original, is mostly considered not to infringe design rights. I have applied a biological similarity, so-called mimicry, to the food market and shown a positive effect from similar foods for all producers, an effect corresponding to the effects of Müllerian mimicry. Expanding a grouping with similar foods creates mutual positive externalities, supporting their legality. There has

4 MARKETS OF QUASI-CREDENCE AND SIMILAR FOODS 81

been no previous explanation of legality from an economic perspective, and what is legal or not in terms of similar products is a problem. A clue to answering the question may be the existence of a mutual positive externality. If consumers consider a similar food as an imitation, a negative externality arises and social welfare decreases with new entries into a market. In such cases, authorities (should) judge the food as an imitation and ban its production. I saw many similar processed foods in Asia and considered the market, and this consideration should also apply to markets in developed countries.

APPENDIX

Appendix 4.1 Proof of Proposition 4.1.

At the equilibrium,

$$q^{O*} = \frac{\bar{v}}{2} - \frac{t^O - t^C}{2(t^O - \gamma t^C)}, \quad q^{C*} = \frac{1}{2(t^O - \gamma t^C)} \left\{ (\bar{v} + 1)t^O - (\gamma \bar{v} + 1)t^C \right\} - \underline{v},$$

$$p^{O*} = \frac{1+\bar{v}}{2}t^O + \frac{1-\gamma\bar{v}}{2}t^C, \text{ and } p^{C*} = t^C.$$

The effects of γ on social welfare are as follows,

$$\frac{d\text{SW}^D}{d\gamma} = \frac{d(\text{CS}^O + \text{CS}^C)}{d\gamma} = \left\{ \left(\gamma_t{}^C \tilde{v} - t^C \right) - \left(t^O \tilde{v} - p^{O*} \right) \right\} \frac{d\tilde{v}}{d\gamma} - (\bar{v} - \tilde{v}) \frac{dp^{O*}}{d\gamma} + \frac{1}{2} t^C (\tilde{v}^2 - \underline{v}^2)$$

$$= \underbrace{\left(U_i^C \Big|_{v_i = \tilde{v}} - U_i^O \Big|_{v_i = \tilde{v}} \right)}_{0} \underbrace{- (\bar{v} - \tilde{v}) \frac{dp^{O*}}{d\gamma}}_{-} = \underbrace{-(\bar{v} - \tilde{v}) \frac{dp^{O*}}{d\gamma}}_{-} + \frac{1}{2} t^C (\tilde{v}^2 - \underline{v}^2) > 0,$$

$$\frac{d\text{SW}}{d\gamma} = \frac{d\pi^{O*}}{d\gamma} + \frac{d(\text{CS}^O + \text{CS}^C)}{d\gamma} = \frac{d((p^{O*} - t^O)q^{O*})}{d\gamma} + \frac{d(\text{CS}^O + \text{CS}^C)}{d\gamma}$$

$$= \left(\frac{dp^{O*}}{d\gamma} q^{O*} + (p^{O*} - t^O) \frac{dq^{O*}}{d\gamma} \right) - (\bar{v} - \tilde{v}) \frac{dp^{O*}}{d\gamma} + \frac{1}{2} t^C (\tilde{v}^2 - \underline{v}^2)$$

$$= \underbrace{\left\{ q^{O*} - (\bar{v} - \tilde{v}) \right\}}_{0} \frac{dp^{O*}}{d\gamma} + (p^{O*} - t^O) \frac{dq^{O*}}{d\gamma} + \frac{1}{2} t^C (\tilde{v}^2 - \underline{v}^2)$$

$$= \underbrace{(p^{O*} - t^O)}_{+} \underbrace{\frac{dq^{O*}}{d\gamma}}_{-} + \frac{1}{2} t^C (\tilde{v}^2 - \underline{v}^2).$$

$$\square$$

82 K. DOMON

Appendix 4.2 Proof of Proposition 4.2.

$$
\begin{aligned}
\frac{d\text{SW}}{d\gamma} &= \frac{d\pi^{O*}}{d\gamma} + \frac{d\left(\text{CS}^{O} + \text{CS}^{C}\right)}{d\gamma} = \frac{d\left(\left(p^{O*} - t^{O}\right)q^{O*}\right)}{d\gamma} + \frac{d\left(\text{CS}^{O} + \text{CS}^{C}\right)}{d\gamma} \\
&= \left(\frac{dp^{O*}}{d\gamma}q^{O*} + \left(p^{O*} - t^{O}\right)\frac{dq^{O*}}{d\gamma}\right) \\
&\quad + \left\{\left(U_i^{C}\Big|_{\substack{v_i=\tilde{v} \\ \gamma=1}} - U_i^{O}\Big|_{v_i=\tilde{v}}\right)\frac{d\tilde{v}}{d\gamma} - q^{O*}\frac{dp^{O*}}{d\gamma}\right\} \\
&= \underbrace{\left(p^{O*} - t^{O}\right)}_{+}\underbrace{\frac{dq^{O*}}{d\gamma}}_{-} + \underbrace{\left(U_i^{C}\Big|_{\substack{v_i=\tilde{v} \\ \gamma=1}} - U_i^{O}\Big|_{v_i=\tilde{v}}\right)}_{-}\underbrace{\frac{d\tilde{v}}{d\gamma}}_{+} < 0. \qquad \square
\end{aligned}
$$

REFERENCES

Anania, G., & Nisticò, R. (2004). Public Regulation as a Substitute for Trust in Quality Food Markets: What If the Trust Substitute Cannot Be Fully Trusted? *Journal of Institutional and Theoretical Economics, 160*(4), 681–701.

Baroncelli, B. E., Fink, C., & Javorcik, S. B. (2005). The Global Distribution of Trademarks: Some Stylised Facts. *World Economy, 28*(6), 765–782.

Bonroy, O., & Constantatos, C. (2008). On the Use of Labels in Credence Goods Markets. *Journal of Regulatory Economics, 33*(3), 237–252.

Darby, R. M., & Karni, E. (1973). Free Competition and the Optimal Amount of Fraud. *Journal of Law and Economics, 16*(1), 67–88.

Domon, K., Ramello, G. B., & Melcrne, A. (2018). *Fake but Original (Original Fake)?* Mimeo: Japanese Food in Southeast Asian Countries.

Fulton, M., & Giannakas, K. (2004). Inserting GM Products into the Food Chain: The Market and Welfare Effects of Different Labeling and Regulatory Regimes. *American Journal of Agricultural Economics, 86*(1), 42–60.

Gabszewicz, J., & Grilo, I. (1992). Price Competition When Consumers Are Uncertain About Which Firm Sells Which Quality. *Journal of Economics and Management Strategy, 1*(4), 629–650.

Giannakas, K. (2002). Information Asymmetries and Consumption Decisions in Organic Food Product Markets. *Canadian Journal of Agricultural Economics, 50*(1), 35–50.

Godinho, M. M., & Ferreira, V. (2012). Analyzing the Evidence of an IPR Take-off in China and India. *Research Policy, 41*(3), 499–511.

Higgins, S. R., & Rubin, P. H. (1986). Counterfeit Goods. *Journal of Law and Economics, 29*(2), 211–230.

Landes, M. W., & Posner, A. R. (1987). Trademark Law: An Economic Perspective. *Journal of Law and Economics, 30*(2), 265–309.

Mealem, Y., Yacobi, Y., & Yaniv, G. (2010). Trademark Infringement and Optimal Monitoring Policy. *Journal of Economics and Business, 62*(2), 116–128.

Ohzaki, N. (2009). *Gitaino Shinka* (in Japanese). Japan: Kaiyusha.

Ruxton, G. D., Sherratt, T. N., & Speed, M. P. (2004). *Avoiding Attack: The Evolutionary Ecology of Crypsis, Warning Signals and Mimicry*. Oxford: Oxford University Press.

Vázquez, F. J., & Watt, R. (2011). Copyright Piracy as Prey-Predator Behavior. *Journal of Bioeconomics, 13*(1), 31–43.

Vetter, H., & Karantininis, K. (2002). Moral Hazard, Vertical Integration, and Public Monitoring in Credence Goods. *European Review of Agricultural Economics, 29*(2), 271–279.

CHAPTER 5

General Conclusions

Abstract This chapter describes several suggestive scenes that I experienced during field research. They are not directly related to my discussions in the previous chapters, but indicate that tackling intellectual property rights (IPR) infringement involves a wide range of considerations, and that researchers in developed countries are likely to misunderstand real situations of counterfeit trade.

Keywords Bribery · Cultural interaction · Informal sector

This monograph indicates differences in intellectual property rights (IPR) infringement between developing and developed countries. When I first started field research in Vietnam, I thought that the research would finish in a year at the most. However, I have intermittently continued researching the subject for almost a decade. The research has remained fascinating not because the market was filled with counterfeits, but because I have found that I can see actual trades and incentives for supplying and demanding counterfeits without enforcement and in settings substantially without meaningful IPRs. I have realized that researchers in developed countries often misunderstand what happens in cases of IPR infringement in Asia. Simple assumptions that they are likely to make can obscure factors that are important to analysis of counterfeiting.

© The Author(s) 2018

K. Domon, *An Economic Analysis of Intellectual Property Rights Infringement*, Palgrave Studies in Institutions, Economics and Law, https://doi.org/10.1007/978-3-319-90466-5_5

In concluding this monograph, I shall add a few scenes that took place behind my field research. When I first visited Vietnam with my college students, two local assistants helped us. They could not understand my purpose for research and wondered at my request to find illegal stores dealing in pirated music CDs. They replied to my email that all the stores to which they usually went sold pirated copies. My experience in Japan seemed nonsensical in Vietnam.

Sellers in CD stores said in interviews that the police sometimes enforced anti-counterfeiting laws, but only fined violators. They could keep the pirated CDs and continue business. In developing countries, we often see cases in which the police make pocket money from the role of enforcing illegal activities and are even involved in crimes. Illegal CD stores seem to be necessary for the police in a certain sense. A similar case was seen in the import of Japanese foods. In Indonesia, staff in Japanese restaurants complained about local customs officials who often arbitrarily changed food regulations to restrict imports. Since the restaurants could not provide dishes without specific foodstuffs, importers had to bribe the officials. What seemed an arbitrary change of restrictions was a device to increase the take from bribes.

In Mexico, I asked local assistants to take me to Tepito, which is the largest black market and the most dangerous area in Latin America. The persons I initially approached to be assistants refused my request, but later I did find people who took me there, even though one driver left during my research and stranded us in the town. There were many wholesalers, selling piles of pirated CDs and other copied products. From interviews with sellers in Mexico, I understood that the informal sector engaging in supplying pirated products depends on illegal business because they cannot find jobs in the formal sector. Behind the illegal business, there is very high income inequality and an inflexible job market. I saw a college student studying at the National Autonomous University of Mexico, the top university in Mexico, who was living in a slum and often eating garbage in the street. She said that she could not find a normal job because she came from the slums and had no relationship with industries. In such a social structure, government is neither inclined nor able to enforce strictly against infringement of IPRs. The Gini index in Latin America is higher than in Asia, and we can easily verify a positive relationship between the Gini index and piracy rates; that is, poverty is a cause of piracy.[1]

When I interviewed Vietnamese college students who used motorcycles daily as transportation, they frankly answered my question as to why they bought counterfeit spare parts. They said that they did not mind receiving spare parts because repair shops explained the quality of the part accurately, no matter whether they used fake packaging. The answer was a puzzle for me, since I could not understand why the fake package was so pervasive and necessary. After I interviewed several times, I again questioned them about why they did not want to buy domestic spare parts. All said that in general they did not trust the quality of domestic industrial products. They unconsciously avoided national brand names. The general reputation of a country affects counterfeiting. This fact could be difficult to find only from questionnaires.

I add another example to show the importance of field research. In researching Japanese food, I ate many Japanese dishes at restaurants with local assistants. They enjoyed this research because they could eat various Japanese dishes, which they usually could not afford, for free. Sushi is very popular in Asia. When I ate sushi at a popular local chain restaurant, my assistant was satisfied with the taste and quality. However, for me the quality was lower than that of cheap sushi sold in supermarkets in Japan. I realized that ordinary local people did not know the authentic taste of sushi. This suggests that quality of food—as consumers estimate it—is subjective, especially in cases where objective criteria for comparison cannot be established.

Almost a decade ago, in Taiwan, I was shocked when a college student who guided me sang Japanese pop music in Japanese, dancing in front of me. She could neither understand nor speak Japanese, but her Japanese singing was perfect. At that time, I was doing research on P2P file-sharing. However, if I understood Chinese, I could have downloaded and watched TV content with subtitles without P2P software soon after it was broadcast in Japan and other Asian countries. This was before YouTube had come to span the globe. This March (in 2018) I visited Vietnam and talked with several college students. All these students

---

[1] From piracy data of the International Intellectual Property Alliance (IIPA), GDP per capita, and the Gini index, we can see a positive effect of the Gini index on piracy rates.

watched Japanese anime on websites for free. The archives of such websites are astonishing, allowing one to watch almost all Japanese anime series with Vietnamese subtitles. An interesting phenomenon is that consumers in foreign countries become interested through such illegal content, and this creates future benefits for the countries pirated from. So we cannot ignore the social impacts of illegal contents on international relationships and cultural interactions.

These episodes describe a part of my experiences in field research that cannot be obtained from data and papers. Since it is impossible to take into account all (potentially) available information, we must choose and focus on important factors, neglecting others that seem less essential. However, field research often changes what we may consider to be the important factors, revealing new ones. This dynamic generally goes undetected by researchers who have never done field research. I hope that this monograph can influence other researchers of Law and Economics (LE) and Industrial Organization (IO) studying in offices and laboratories.

INDEX

A
Anania, G., 63
Andersen, B., 15
ASEAN, 2, 68
Asymmetric Digital Subscriber Line (ADSL), 12, 19, 29
Asymmetric information, 37, 64, 65

B
Backward induction, 50
Bain, J.S., 3
Bandwagon effect, 56
Banerjee, A.V., 4
Barker, G., 15
Baroncelli, B.E., 69
Batesian mimicry, 70
Becker, G.S., 3
Besen, S.M., 15
Bonroy, O., 63
BRICs, 2

C
Chow, D., 36

Coase, R.H., 3
Cobb-Douglas utility function, 31
Constantatos, C., 63
Consumers' surplus, 44–46, 67, 69, 72, 80
Copy control CD, 17
Copyright, 4, 7, 12, 14, 16–19, 21, 22, 24–26, 28, 32, 33, 71
Counterfeit, 2, 5, 6, 8, 9, 36–40, 42, 47–57, 62–66, 68, 69, 74, 78–80, 85, 87
Counterfeiter, 2, 8, 36, 38–40, 48, 49, 52–55, 57, 63, 74, 80
Counterfeit food, 7, 8, 62–65, 67, 69
Counterfeiting game, 48, 51, 54
Credence goods, 8, 37, 38, 62, 67–69, 80
Credence quality, 62–64
Credence service, 38

D
Darby, R.M., 37, 62
Deceptive counterfeit, 63
Design right, 8, 70, 74, 80

© The Editor(s) (if applicable) and The Author(s) 2018
K. Domon, *An Economic Analysis of Intellectual Property Rights Infringement*, Palgrave Studies in Institutions, Economics and Law,
https://doi.org/10.1007/978-3-319-90466-5

90 INDEX

Digital rights management (DRM), 12, 17
Dixit-Stiglitz's CES utility function, 74
Doi Moi, 36
Dominant strategy, 51
Domon, K., 11, 15, 17
Duflo, E., 4
Dulleck, U., 38

E
Economics of transaction cost, 3
European Union's Asia IT&C Programme, 19

F
Fair use, 14
Fake food, 8
Fake package, 7, 39, 42, 47, 56, 87
Fake spare parts, 7, 35, 47
Ferreira, V., 69
Field research, 4–9, 18, 21, 27, 62, 85–88
Fink, C., 69
Fleisch, E., 37
Food processing machine, 69, 70
Fraud, 37
Frenz, M., 15
FTTH, 29
Fujita, M., 36
Fulton, M., 63

G
Gabszewicz, J., 63
Generic modified food, 66
Giannakas, K., 62, 63
Gini index, 86
Gnutella, 12
Godinho, M.M., 69

Gordon, W.J., 14
Granzin, K.L., 37
Grilo, I., 63
Grossman, G.M., 38, 56

H
Helper, S., 6
Higgins, S.R., 38, 62
Hoecht, A., 37
Hung, C.L., 36

I
Illegal product, 5, 28
Illegal trade, 6
IMF, 18
Imitated food, 8, 69
Imitation, 8, 32, 39, 67, 71, 73, 74, 77, 81
Import-substitution policy, 36
Incomplete information, 15, 38–40, 42–45, 47, 48, 62, 64–66, 68, 69, 77
Industrial Organization (IO), 3, 4, 8, 9, 88
Intellectual Property Rights (IPR), 2, 3, 5, 85, 86
International Intellectual Property Alliance (IIPA), 28, 87
International Telecommunication Union, 19
ISDN, 19
ISP, 19–21, 28, 32
i-Tunes, 12, 28

J
Japan External Trade Organization (JETRO), 2
Javorcik, S.B., 69

K

Kaikati, J.G., 37
Karantininis, K., 63
Karni, E., 37, 62
Kerschbamer, R., 38
Kimizuka, M., 32
Kirby, S.N., 15

L

LaGarce, R., 37
Landes, W.N., 74
Law and Economics (LE), 3, 4, 8, 9, 88
Leibenstein, H., 56
Liebowitz, S.J., 15
Lofland, J., 6
Lofland, L.H., 6

M

Maloney, T., 15
Mealem, Y., 74
Methodology, 2, 4, 8
Miceli, T.J., 4
Mimicry, 8, 70, 71, 80
Mimic(s), 8, 70, 71
Minagawa, T., 37
Mislabelling, 63
Monopolistic competition, 76
Mortimer, J.M., 16, 24
MP3, 12, 17, 20
Müllerian mimicry, 73, 80

N

Nakamura, K., 11
Napster, 12, 15
Nash equilibrium, 25, 38, 43, 49–51, 56, 72
National Autonomous University of Mexico, 86

Negative frequency-dependent selection, 69, 71, 73
Nisticò, R., 63
Non-deceptive counterfeit, 62, 65
Nosko, C., 16, 24

O

Ohkuma, S., 2
Ohzaki, N., 70
Olsen, J.E., 37
Opportunity cost, 16, 17, 21, 31, 32

P

P2P file sharing, 7, 12, 15–23, 27–29, 31–33, 87
Piracy rate, 13, 28, 87
Pirated CD, 6, 7, 13, 18, 19, 21, 22, 24, 26–28, 31, 86
Positive frequency-dependent selection, 73
Positive mutual externality, 73
Posner, R.A., 74
Predator, 70, 71, 73
Price discrimination, 14, 15, 62, 63
Product differentiation, 8, 30, 74

Q

Quasi-credence food, 66–69

R

Ramello, G.B., 38
Recording Industry Association of America (RIAA), 4
Risk aversion, 63
Rubin, P.H., 38, 62
Ruxton, G.D., 70

92 INDEX

S
Sato, I., 6
Shapiro, C., 38, 56
Sherratt, T.N., 70
Similar food, 61, 71, 73, 80, 81
Snob effect, 38, 62
Sorensen, M., 16, 24
Speed, M.P., 70
Spotify, 12
Staake, T., 37
Stigler, J.G., 3
Sub-game perfect Nash equilibrium, 51, 53

T
Tepito, 86
Thiesse, F., 37
Threshold of market existence, 73
Tirole J., 3
Trademark, 7, 8, 36, 38, 49, 57, 69, 70, 74
Trott, P., 37
Two-sided incomplete information, 65, 66

U
UNESCO, 18
United States Trade Representative (USTR), 2

US Special 301 Report, 18
U.S. Trade Act, 2

V
Varian, H.R., 15, 16
Veblen effect, 56
Vertical integration, 63
Vetter, H., 63
Video cassette recorder (VCR), 14

W
Watt, R., 71
World Bank, 55
World Trade Organization (WTO), 2

Y
Yacobi, Y., 74
Yamazaki, N., 17
Yaniv, G., 74
YouTube, 13, 87